AMERICAN PHILOSOPHICAL
QUARTERLY
MONOGRAPH SERIES

Edited by Nicholas Rescher

STUDIES IN ETHICS

Essays by:

Charles V. Blatz   R. L. Franklin

Claudia Card   James D. Wallace

Norman O. Dahl   A. D. Woozley

D1115343

Monograph No. 7   Oxford, 1973

PUBLISHED BY BASIL BLACKWELL

© *American Philosophical Quarterly 1973*
ISBN 0 631 11510 2

Library of Congress Catalog
Card No.: 72-85668

PRINTED IN ENGLAND
by C. Tinling & Co. Ltd., London and Prescot

AMERICAN PHILOSOPHICAL QUARTERLY
MONOGRAPH SERIES

CONTENTS

EDITOR'S PREFACE

This is the seventh in the Monograph Series inaugurated by the *American Philosophical Quarterly* in 1967. It is once more a collection of articles—the recruitment of suitable monographs proper having regrettably proved a matter of greater difficulty than anticipated.

This is the second such anthology in the area of ethics and moral philosophy, a fact which attests to the current vitality of the discipline. The essays collected together here exemplify a variety of approaches within the broad sphere of analytical methodology. The *American Philosophical Quarterly* is most grateful to the learned contributors for permitting the inclusion of their essays in this collection.

The editor acknowledges with thanks the collaboration of his wife, who assisted in editing the work and in seeing it through the press.

Nicholas Rescher
Pittsburgh
April, 1972

Mitigating and Meliorating Defenses

CHARLES V. BLATZ

1. INTRODUCTION

TWO sorts of excuses which relieve us of blame for doing something morally wrong, or for failing to do what morally ought to be done, have been recognized. Exculpating excuses relieve us of all blame for such moral failings. Mitigating defenses only reduce the amount of blame of which it is morally justifiable for us to be made the object. We do not understand enough about the functioning of mitigating defenses. And as a direct consequence, the way has been opened for a basic misunderstanding of exculpating excuses.

I want to do three things here. First, I want to show the necessity of distinguishing two very different sorts of defenses which might be called "mitigating defenses." I shall call these "mitigating" and "meliorating defenses." Second, I shall offer analyses of these and two additional related sorts of defenses. Third, I want to show that an understanding of meliorating defenses provides us with reason both for rejecting one analysis of exculpating excuses, and for accepting a competing analysis.

There are two ways in which the discussion will be simplified. First, we shall speak of defenses against blame for states of affairs. Second, our concern will be with states of affairs which are morally untoward.

The sense of "state of affairs" which I have in mind is rather more inclusive than usual. It should be clear that we are justifiably blamed for doing certain things, and for failing to do or omitting doing others, such as: causing embarrassment or mental anguish in another, killing another, failing to keep a promise, and failing to help another in need. Also, we might be said to be justifiably blamed for states of others such as: their embarrassment, mental anguish, death, or misfortune in a time of need. Let us call "states of affairs," such things as someone's kicking a football, sampling a wine, lying to or embarrassing another, failing to keep a promise, neglecting his wife, and killing another. That is, I propose that we speak of the referent of any verbal phrase including a participial form of a verb of action as a state of affairs. As well, of course, we shall use "state of affairs" in the more traditional way to speak of an object having a certain property. We

1

shall then be able to speak of a defense against blame for a certain state of affairs, S, and our remarks will cover both of the relevant sorts of things.[1]

We are justifiably blamed for various sorts of failing: legal, professional, moral, and so on. Our concern is with blame for states of affairs in which something has gone wrong morally. Let us call any state of affairs "morally untoward," if it would not have been produced, had the relevant person not done something morally wrong or something he morally ought not to have done, in some sense. It might be held that such a state is one which resulted from our failing to do what we actually ought to have done, or *prima facie* ought to have done, and so on. For our purposes here, we need not determine in what way(s) an S must be morally untoward for someone to be justifiably blamed for it. Whatever the way(s) in question, that is the relevant sense(s) of "morally untoward."

2. LEGAL ANALOGUES

If we simply say that mitigating excuses relieve the relevant person, P, of some, but not all justifiable blame, we shall cloud over a necessary distinction between two sorts of defenses which might be considered mitigating. The following two questions indicate this difference. Do mitigating excuses relieve P of some, but not all blame for the state he is charged with producing? Or, do they relieve P of any blame he might have incurred by producing S, while, at the same time, they indicate he is, or might be, blameworthy to a lesser degree for some other, less untoward state of affairs which he brought about in the circumstances? Evidently, each of these questions would be answered "yes" when asked about different mitigating defenses given in a court of law. This is one of the points H. L. A. Hart makes in his "Prolegomenon to the Principles of Punishment." Hart labels the two sorts of pleas in question, defenses of "informal" and "formal mitigation," respectively:

> In the first case the law fixes a maximum penalty and leaves it to the judge to give such weight as he thinks proper, in selecting the punishment to be applied to a particular offender, to (among other considerations) mitigating factors. It is here that the barrister makes his "plea in mitigation." Sometimes however legal rules provide that the presence of a mitigating factor shall always remove the offense into a separate category carrying a lower maximum penalty. This is "formal" mitigation and the most

[1] We shall not be concerned here with defenses against blame for failing to be some way we morally ought to be; only with defenses for failing (morally) in the states we produce.

prominent example of it is Provocation which in English law is operative only in relation to homicide. Provocation is not a matter of Justification or Excuse for it does not exclude conviction or punishment; but "reduces" the charges from murder to manslaughter and the possible maximum penalty from death to life imprisonment.[2]

We do not have to look very hard to find defenses against blame for moral failings analogous to defenses of formal and informal mitigation before the law. *P* is defending himself against blame for the untoward *S* of lying to a friend about what a third party has said of the friend. His defense makes it clear that *P* did not pay proper attention to what the third party said and, consequently, misinterpreted him. It is generally recognized that to lie is, roughly, to intentionally convey false "information." *P*'s defense, then, would function like a defense of formal mitigation. It would show *P* is *not* blameworthy for *S* (since he did not produce it), but, perhaps for the other, lesser offense of conveying information carelessly gathered. This moral *analogue* is only that. In such cases, we do not work with an institutionalized codification of the circumstances which reduce a charge. Still, what is going on in the case in question is very like what goes on in offering successful pleas of formal mitigation.

Also, there are defenses against blame for moral failings analogous to informal mitigation defenses. Suppose the charge is that of conveying misinformation about, and to a friend, and thereby upsetting him, *S*. *P* shows he made some small effort to get the information straight and he thought that he had done so. Here, the defense does *not* show that *P* did not produce *S*, but only some less untoward state. Still, it relieves him of *some blame*. We would probably say this. Because *P*'s getting the information wrong did involve his making some effort to avoid getting incorrect "information," he is not worthy of as much blame for *S* as he would be, if he had not tried at all. But, as *P* would have gotten it right had he tried a little harder, he is worthy of some blame for the relevant state. As in the cases of informal mitigation before the law, we (the judges) are here taking a certain circumstance into account (*P*'s making some effort), and accordingly adjust the amount of blame *P* is justifiably accorded *for the S he is charged with producing*.

There are not institutionalized statements of maximum penalties which we can follow in such cases. Still, this difference between legal informal mitigation and the moral analogue should not make us fail to see the similarities.

[2] H. L. A. Hart, "Prolegomenon to the Principles of Punishment" in *Punishment and Responsibility*, ed. by H. L. A. Hart (New York, 1968), p. 15.

I want to analyze the moral analogues of formal and informal mitigation before the law. For this purpose, let us adopt the following terminology. The phrase "*mitigating* defense" will be used for any moral analogue of what Hart calls a defense of *formal* mitigation. For the analogue of a defense of *informal* mitigation, the phrase "meliorating defense" will be used.

3. MITIGATING DEFENSES

What can be said by way of a general characterization of mitigating defenses? The example in which *P* is accused of lying to a friend is suggestive. *P*'s mitigating defense was that he had (out of carelessness) misunderstood the source of his "information" and had conveyed it without knowing it was false. This defense works as follows. It shows that *P* did not produce the relevant *S*, because it shows a condition necessary for correctly describing what he did as '*S*,' was absent in the circumstances. *P* did not intend to deceive. At the same time, it indicates that *P* can justifiably be charged with producing some other state, *S'*, less untoward than the *S* he was charged with producing. He was careless where a friend's interests were at stake. These points suggest the following analysis.

A defense *d* is a mitigating defense against a charge that *P* produced a particular morally untoward state *S* (for which he is blameworthy) if and only if:

(a) *d* shows that *P* brought about some state of affairs *S'*,
(b) *d* and any other true statement *s* (but not *s* alone) imply that there was some circumstance *C* present at the time of *P*'s production of *S'*,
(c) the absence of *C* is a logically necessary condition for the occurrence of *S*,
(d) *S'* is less morally untoward than *S*, and is morally untoward in such a way that *P* might be morally blameworthy for it.

Conditions (a), (b), and (c) reflect the fact that mitigating defenses show that *P* brought about a state incompatible with the one he is accused of producing. Condition (d) reflects the fact that they might be said to reduce the charge against *P*. *P* is left facing lesser charges; charges of bringing about a less untoward state.

Two of the four conditions should be relatively clear. Condition (b) needs comment. Why is it stated *d and* any other true statement *s imply* that some *C* was present? What is meant is this. There is a relation between *d* and *s* such that when they are true, a statement to effect that some *C* was present at the time of *P*'s production of *S'* is also true. This allows for a defense, such as lack of intention to deceive, to be mitigating against the charge of lying. Here, we would probably say the defense *entails* that a circumstance, the absence of which is necessary to lying, was present. But this use of "imply" also allows a defense of carelessness in gathering information to be a mitigating defense against blame for lying. There is no contradiction in saying P was careless in gathering information he passed on and he lied in passing the information. But, if P's defense against blame for lying was that he was careless in gathering that information (d), and it is also true that passing on just the information he did can be attributed solely to carelessness (s), then we would say his defense was mitigating. It then would be reasonable to believe that there was no intent to deceive and so, no lying.

Condition (b) needs a further comment. It was stated in terms of d and s implying that some C was present *at the time of P's production of S'*, not that C was part of or a factor in P's production of S'. Were we to say that C was a part of or a factor in P's production of S', this might suggest that C must be such that we would correctly mention it in describing the necessary and sufficient conditions of that production. Such a circumstance might be P's intention in doing what he did, certain of the beliefs he held while doing what he did, and so on. With C specified in this way, the analysis would cover some of the cases it should. It would allow lack of intention to deceive to provide P with a mitigating defense against blame for lying. But it would not cover all the cases we would count as mitigating defenses. For example, suppose P is defending himself against blame for failing to keep a promise to help a friend in need. His defense is that he had never promised, though he ought to have helped. This would be mitigating in spite of the fact that we would not say his *not* having made a promise was a circumstance which was present in or a factor of P's production of the state he brought about. The proposed statement of (b) seems desirable.

Condition (d) also needs comment. It might be thought that this part of the analysis is unacceptable. Should it not be worded so that P is said to be blameworthy for the less untoward S'? No. Surely, someone can offer a successful mitigating plea, and still show he is not worthy of blame for the "lesser offense." In the previous example, P could offer what we would call a mitigating defense by showing he made no promise to help. And, he might point out he would not be justifiably blamed for not helping because he was physically unable to do so.

Condition (d) as stated allows for such a possibility. And, it allows for the possibility that the only thing P can do in his own defense is to get the charge reduced.[3] The proposed analysis is called for. Let us now contrast mitigating defenses with a different, but resembling defense against blame for a morally untoward S.

The defenses in question operate, in all ways, like a mitigating defense, except they do not show that P produced some state less untoward than the one he is accused of producing. Two examples of such defenses are the following. First, P is defending himself against blame for the morally untoward state of making someone's acquaintance only to use him as a source of information valuable to P. His defense is that he was introduced by a third party, immediately took a liking to the man, and subsequently sought out the pleasure of his acquaintance's company. The defense would be successful, for it shows the presence of some circumstance which must be absent before P could even have produced the S he is charged with. It shows P lacked any interest in meeting the man only to use him. But, the defense does not show P produced any S' less untoward than S. Second, P is facing the charge that he broke a promise to attend a dinner party. He shows that he said he might drop in, but that he had not promised to do so. The defense makes it clear that a condition logically necessary for P's having produced S is absent. But it does not leave P facing a lesser charge, as would a mitigating defense. Both mitigating defenses, and those in question now, fully relieve P of blame for a certain S by showing he did not produce that S. Mitigating defenses leave P facing another charge. Those in question now do not. Let us call defenses of this latter sort, "logically exculpating defenses." We can characterize them in a way similar to the way we characterized mitigating defenses.

A defense d is a logically exculpating defense against a charge that P produced a particular morally untoward state S (for which he is blameworthy) if and only if:

(a) d and any other true statement s (but not s alone) imply that there was some circumstance C present at the time of P's alleged production of S,

(b) the absence of C is a logically necessary condition for the occurrence of S,

(c) d does not show that P brought about some state of affairs S' which is untoward.

[3] It should be noted that mitigating defenses seem to be analogous to their legal counterparts on this point. In the passage quoted above, Hart implies that acceptance of a mitigating defense does not mean that the relevant party will be convicted and justifiably punished on the lesser charge. The same seems to be true in American criminal law. This is made clear in Judge Pound's opinion in the New York appelate court decision in the case of the People vs. Koerber, cited in *Moral Duty and Legal Responsibility*, ed. by Philip E. Davis (New York, 1966), pp. 73–80.

This brief look at logically exculpating defenses will suffice for present purposes.[4] Let us now turn to meliorating defenses.

4. MELIORATING DEFENSES

We have seen one example of a meliorating defense. This is the case in which P was defending himself against blame for upsetting his friend (F) with misinformation. The charge would be that *P is blameworthy for upsetting F by conveying misinformation.* P might have said to F that a third party was disgusted with F because of the way he left his wife. However, the third party in fact said only that he was upset that the couple had broken up. A defense which would *reduce P's* blame for upsetting F by conveying misinformation would be that P made some attempt to get the information right, but did not make the attempt which he and any normal person could have made and which would have ended in his getting the story straight. P might answer the charge in this way by saying: "Admittedly, I did not get the story straight when I could have; but I did listen to the other person, even if I did not do so very carefully."

It would be helpful to set out briefly two more cases of defenses of this type. P is defending himself against the charge that he is *blameworthy for shooting and wounding someone else.* His defense is that on the basis of an admittedly cursory examination, he judged that the gun was a toy, not a real weapon. Suppose P and another come upon a weapon in the other's house. P picks it up making a cursory examination of it and pulls the trigger having aimed at the other person in play. In such a case, P might again try to make the best of what is, for him, a bad situation by entering the following plea: "Well, I did only give it a quick once-over, but, at least I did that much."

The third case is this. P is defending himself against the charge that he is *blameworthy for injuring a friend's reputation by revealing a confidence to the town gossip G.* P points out that, in his judgment, it seemed safe to tell G, though the defense makes it clear that P did not do what he very easily could have done; he did not check with others to determine the discretion of G. The plea could be this: "I, of course, did not check around about how discreet G is, but it seemed all right to trust him." We might also imagine that G was only a slight

---

[4] What I am calling "logically exculpating defenses" might be what Joel Feinberg has in mind when he speaks of "defeating excuses." "If the 'defeating' excuse is accepted, the fault-imputation *must* be withdrawn; this is what it means for a fault-imputation to be defeasible, and it allows for us to show that 'cheat,' 'murder,' and 'lie,' are defeasible faults." Joel Feinberg, "Action and Responsibility" in *The Philosophy of Action*, ed. by Alan R. White (London, 1968), p. 98.

acquaintance of P and that while he had given P no reason to *not* trust his discretion, he had given him no reason to do so either. An examination of these three cases should give us some idea of what is necessary and sufficient to a defense's being meliorating.

First, the defenses in question might function as logically exculpating or mitigating defenses against other charges. However, they function in neither of these ways here. P does not and is not trying to show that he did not produce the states with which he is charged. P is attempting to "get himself off the hook" by showing something about the ways in which he *did* produce the relevant states; by pointing out they were in part due to misunderstanding, a mistake in judgment, and to ignorance that G is a gossip.

A connected point can be made in the following way. Mitigating defenses might be said to change the charge which P must answer if he is to show he would not be justifiably blamed. That is, such defenses leave P facing a charge of being blameworthy for producing a state of affairs described differently from the one mentioned in the original charge. They do this by showing that what P produced falls under another description, *logically incompatible* with that given of the state P is charged with (see clauses (b) and (c)), and that it is a state, the production of which, is less untoward than the production of the state P is charged with producing. Meliorating defenses do not change the charge P must answer.

Consider the case in which the man upset his friend by conveying misinformation. We could say that the defense in this example broadens the description of what P produced to read: "upsetting F by conveying misinformation due to an admittedly avoidable misunderstanding while he was attempting to collect the right information." Under this description, and given the operating moral code, P's production of the relevant S cannot be justifiably met by as much blame as it could if it fit only the description of the charge. (We have yet to explain how this works, of course.) In this way, we could say that meliorating defenses function by *enlarging the description of what P produced from that given in the charge against which he must defend himself.* But this is far different from, in fact is incompatible with, saying that meliorating defenses change the charge in the way mitigating defenses do.

Second, the defenses given in the example (misunderstanding, mistake, and ignorance, respectively), are sometimes exculpating. They can exculpate in a way different from that in which they would exculpate from blame for S if they were logically exculpating or mitigating. Suppose the misunderstanding, mistake, and ignorance were all unavoidable. We would then say P is worthy of no blame at all for the relevant states. The defenses would not show he did not produce the relevant states. Rather, they would show he produced them in circumstances (unavoidable misunderstanding and so on), in the presence of which, the moral code would prohibit blaming P at all. When these defenses are exculpating in this way, we might say they are *normatively exculpating*.

Third, in the examples cited, the defenses are not normatively exculpating. P is still worthy of some blame. The reason is this. In each case, there is an added element, the presence of which attenuates the force of the defense. In the first example, P failed to take that amount of care which would have prevented his getting the information wrong; and which the average person could have taken. In the gun case, P failed to avert making a mistake in his judgment by taking precautions which he, or any normal person, could have taken. In the third case, P failed to make an investigation to find out what was "common knowledge"; namely, that his interlocutor was a gossip. These circumstances attenuate the blame-relieving force of the defense. However, they do not eliminate it completely. In each of the cases, P did make some attempt to get the relevant information. Consequently, he is not blameworthy to the degree to which he would have been had he made no such attempt. But in each case, the presence of the attenuating circumstance (AC) shows his attempt was a poor one.[5]

Fourth, the attenuating circumstance (AC) is such that it need not have been present. I mean that, normally, people can avoid the presence of these (AC)s in their production of states of affairs. If this were not so, then we would say that the excuses in the examples are exculpating and not simply defenses which partially relieve P of blame for the states in question. The presence of the (AC)s attenuates the relevant defenses by showing that had P avoided their presence, he may not have produced any state for which he would be at all blameworthy. This point should suggest another question about the operation of meliorating defenses.

When P offers a successful meliorating defense, what is morally

---

[5] When P produced the relevant states, he was not indifferent with regard to the possible untoward results connected with the attenuating circumstances. Nor, need he have been acting in a way the "average man" or "man of reasonable care" would not have acted. I am not saying that P produced some S where the "man of reasonable care" would not have done so. P failed in these cases where he (and the "average man") *need not* have failed, and that is the main point. According to most understandings of negligence then, the presence of the (AC)s does not indicate negligence in P's production of the relevant states. And, it does not wholly vitiate the force of the defenses the way negligence might. It only weakens or attenuates that force. How this happens we shall understand more fully as we proceed.

B

untoward in the situation? Clearly something is, for he is blame-worthy to some degree for something. But is it the state he produced, or the (AC), or both?

It should be clear that what is untoward, what P is justifiably blamed for, in such cases, are the states in question, not the (AC)s. Consider the gun case where the (AC) is failure to make the proper investigation of the weapon (which he could have made). We do not want to say that such a failure is itself morally untoward. Suppose P fails in this way on a deserted island with the only result being that he startles himself. The failure would not be morally untoward, though, of course, it might have been imprudent. If a man wants to fail to properly investigate what could be a weapon, that is his lookout, as long as the failure would not lead to the production of an untoward state. Similarly, if a man wants to be careless in gathering information he passes on, or not properly investigate the discretion of those he speaks with, and this would not lead to the production of a morally untoward state, then he is (morally) free to do so. Why we might want to say that these (AC)s are themselves untoward is that they have, in the circumstances, led to the production of morally untoward states. We might say they are *instrumentally morally untoward*.

Caution should be exercised in saying this. To say they are instru-mentally morally untoward is, I suggest, to say no more than that they, though themselves not untoward, can bring about states which are morally untoward.[6] This means that the (AC)s are not themselves morally untoward; as should be the case since we are morally free to be imprudent on some occasions. Rather, the blame a meliorating defense leaves is blame for the state in question. (As the (AC) is not itself untoward, it does not seem reasonable to say that P is blame-worthy for S and the (AC).)[7]

Finally, we have seen that the defenses in our examples might be normatively exculpating *or*, in the presence of an (AC) only melio-rating. Can we say that what makes these defenses only meliorating is simply the presence of the (AC)? It is extremely important for us to see why the answer is no.

Consider the gun-injury case. If we held that the presence of an (AC) alone is what makes a defense only meliorating, we would say

---

[6] Compare this with what G. E. Moore said of instrumental goodness. "When-ever we judge that a thing is 'good as a means,' we are making a judgment with regard to its causal relations: we judge *both* that it will have a particular kind of effect, *and* that that effect will be good in itself." G. E. Moore, *Principia Ethica* (Cambridge, 1962), p. 22.

[7] P might be blameworthy for not seeing to the absence of the (AC) as well as for S. But, we are asking what he is really blameworthy for, when he gives his meliorating defense against blame for S.

the defense is meliorating in this example, simply because P's mistake in judgment was the product of an avoidable failure to make the proper investigation of the weapon. But, if we say this I do not see how we can avoid saying the following. Whenever the defense of mistake in judgment is coupled with the added circumstance of avoidable failure to make the proper investigation, the defense can only be meliorating. *This is false*. Suppose our errant P runs up to a man at the station, stops him short and with much back-slapping, and attempted hand pumping, greets a stranger he took for a long lost friend. The "victim" is slightly ill and P's behavior makes him feel worse. The charge would be that P is blameworthy for upsetting a stranger who is ill. P's defense is that he made a mistake in judgment. In such a case, we would say this defense has normatively exculpated P, even though the whole thing might have been easily avoided. The added circumstance was present but its presence did not make the defense meliorating. What makes a defense meliorating, cannot be the presence of the added circumstance alone.

What is missing from the account of what makes a defense meliorating as opposed to normatively exculpating? The answer is: the untowardness of the state with which P is charged. Very simply, the mistake plus (AC) fails to exculpate P from blame for the gun-injury case because too much is at stake; while it does exculpate in the station because so little is at stake.

Blaming P for a moral failing inflicts suffering (as a rule) and is, then justifiable only under certain circumstances. In the two examples in question, we can look at the offering of the defense of mistake (even in the presence of the (AC)) as an attempt to show that blaming in these cases would be infliction of suffering exceeding a justifiable limit. In the station case, it is most natural to say not much has gone wrong (morally) and, after all, mistakes do happen, even avoidable ones. The defense exculpates because the state produced was "not that toward." And to blame P when he brought about the stranger's momentary suffering by mistake (even an avoidable one) would seem overly harsh. The added circumstance is present. But, it does not lower the effectiveness of the defense to the point that blaming for this slight offense would not exceed the limits of justifiable imposition of suffering. We might say it is not strongly attenuating in these circumstances.

In the case of the gun injury, however, the S produced is, comparatively so morally untoward that some blame is justifiable. The (AC) is, here, *strongly attenuating*. It is not, of course, as if P had made no attempt to determine whether the object was a real weapon. He just fell short of making the proper effort.

The point is this. A defense is a meliorating defense partially because of the presence of the (AC). But as well, a defense is made meliorating in part by the untowardness of the state in question.

We can now offer an analysis of meliorating defenses.

A defense d is a meliorating defense against a charge that P produced a particular morally untoward state S (for which he is blameworthy) if and only if:

(a) d and any other true statement s imply that there was a normatively blame-relieving circumstance (Nbr) present at the time of P's production of S (and this is not implied by s alone),

(b) there was an attenuating circumstance (AC) present at the time of P's production of S,

(c) (AC) is strongly attenuating for the particular (Nbr) the presence of which d and s show.

We have simplified the statement of this proposal by using three technical terms. The first order of business is to explicate these.

A circumstance present at the time of P's production of S is a normatively blame-relieving circumstance (Nbr) if and only if the presence of (Nbr) would make it unjustifiable for P to be blamed for S to any extent, assuming (Nbr) is the only circumstance in the situation bearing on P's blameworthiness for S.

An (Nbr) is simply some circumstance which a successful excuse will show was present at the time of production of the relevant S. When it is present alone, it renders P not blameworthy for the morally untoward S he has produced. It does so by being one of the circumstances in the presence of which all blame is rendered unjustifiable by the moral code being used to determine the justifiability of blame. We have said in condition (a) that the (Nbr) is " . . . present at the time of. . . . " We must put it this way, if we are to count as (Nbr)s such circumstances as coercion, which may not properly be said to be *in* P's production of the relevant S.

A circumstance present at the time of P's production of S is a strongly attenuating circumstance (AC) if and only if given the presence of (AC), the untowardness of S, and the presence of some appropriate (Nbr), it would be justifiable for P to be blamed to some degree for S, but not to that degree he might be justifiably blamed if he produced S with no (Nbr) present at the time.

What is "*some appropriate* (Nbr)"? Some (AC)s will have nothing to do with whether a person's defense should be considered exculpating or only partially relieve P of blame. The fact that P failed to make the proper investigation of the gun is relevant to whether his defense

of mistaken judgment of the weapon is exculpating or only meliorating. That *P* also failed to make a proper determination of the discretion of the party injured is not relevant. The (Nbr) in question
(mistake in judgment) is not appropriate for the second (AC) in
question (avoidable failure to examine the other's discretion). Clearly,
a given (Nbr) may be "appropriate" for one (AC) and not for another
on some occasion.

This brings us to the last technical notion.

An attenuating circumstance (AC) is strongly attenuating for a particular
(Nbr) if and only if (AC) would be strongly attenuating assuming (Nbr)
is the only normatively blame-relieving circumstance present at the time
of *P*'s production of *S*.

Normatively exculpating defenses closely resemble meliorating
defenses, but are different in an important respect. After having made
all the investigations a reasonable man would, and concluding the
gun is a toy, *P* injures another with it. His defense is that he did make
all reasonable investigations. Here, there is no (AC) and we would
probably say the defense is exculpating. The moral code by which the
justifiability of blaming *P* for *S* is being determined would say no
blame for the moral failing is justifiable. In this sense, *P*'s defense
would be *normatively exculpating*. The following characterization of
normatively exculpating defenses is indicated.

A defense *d* is a normatively exculpating defense against a charge that *P*
produced a particular morally untoward state *S* (for which he is blameworthy) if and only if:

(a) *d* and any other true statement *s* imply that there was an (Nbr)
present at the time of *P*'s production of *S* (and this is not implied by
s alone),

(b) there was no (AC) present which is strongly attenuating for the (Nbr)
in question.

This suggestion should be clear from previous remarks. Let us now
offer a defense of it, and the previous analysis, against competing
analyses.

5. AN OPPOSING THEORY

The way I have stated the analyses of meliorating and normatively
exculpating defenses should suggest the following: I am contending
that they do not function, respectively, by showing that the relevant
state of affairs was not as untoward as it might have been, or, by
showing it was not untoward at all. That is, I am suggesting that these
defenses do not bear on the untowardness of the relevant *S* at all. Not

all would agree with this contention. And, those who would disagree might wish to object to the analyses in question. Let me describe the position on the basis of which the objection would be made.

It would hold that there are defenses we might call exculpating and partial blame-relieving excuses. It would be agreed that these defenses relieve *P* of blame for *S* by showing it is unjustifiable to blame him for *S*. But, they would say that the way this is done is by the defense showing something about the supposed untowardness of the relevant *S*. A normatively exculpating defense would show that the *S* in question was *not untoward at all*. Consequently, there is nothing for which *P* might be justifiably blamed. A defense which we have called meliorating, shows that *S* was *not as untoward as it might have been*. Consequently, *P* can be justifiably blamed only to a relatively lessened degree. Normatively exculpating defenses, on this account, would nullify the claim that there is anything for which *P* might justifiably be blamed. Let us call this the "nullification account" (NA) of normatively exculpating and meliorating defenses.

The (NA) is not the most popular account of normatively exculpating defenses. It has had some important proponents.[8] But an opposing account does seem to have become more popular.[9] According to this popular account (PA) a normatively exculpating defense shows the presence of some circumstance, given which the relevant normative code prohibits blaming *P* for *S*, *even though S* was untoward. The analysis I have given of meliorating and normatively exculpating defenses is a (PA) account. Defenses of these two sorts were said to differ by the presence of the (AC) and the *relative untowardness of the states in question*.

The (PA) account does not preclude the possibility of there being defenses of the sort the (NA) spoke about. Proponents of the (PA) would say there are such defenses, but, for clarity, we should call them justifications (and partial justifications) to mark their difference from normatively exculpating defenses (and meliorating defenses). In short, an (NA) analysis of normatively exculpating and meliorating defenses would treat them as justifications. Any (PA) analysis of these pleas would distinguish them from justifications.

An (NA) theorist might object to any (PA) proposals by holding

[8] See, e.g.: Thomas Hobbes, *Leviathan*, ed. by Michael Oakeshott (New York, 1962), pp. 222–223; Alexander Sesonske, *Value and Obligation* (New York, 1964), pp. 79 and 86.

[9] See, e.g.: John L. Austin, "A Plea for Excuses" in *Philosophical Papers*, ed. by J. O. Urmson and G. J. Warnock (Oxford, 1961), p. 124; and Richard B. Brandt, "A Utilitarian Theory of Excuses," *The Philosophical Review*, vol. 78 (1969), pp. 339–340.

that they fail to treat the relevant defenses as justifications. I want to support these analyses by showing we must accept the (PA), not the (NA).

The (NA) is unacceptable because no (NA) analysis can explain why a defense is meliorating, in that it is only partially blame relieving, instead of exculpating. I have argued that a defense is meliorating, and not exculpating, for two reasons: the presence of an (AC), and the relative untowardness of the S in question. But, no (NA) theory can explain the difference in this way.

The (NA) theory makes the untowardness of the relevant S dependent upon whether a normatively exculpating or meliorating defense (or no defense at all) can be offered. If a normatively exculpating defense can be offered, the S in question would be shown, thereby, to be *not untoward at all*. If only the meliorating defense can be offered, the S in question would be shown, thereby, to be *not as untoward as it might have been*. (If no such defense can be offered, presumably the S would be as untoward as it might be.) *Whether or to what degree the relevant S is untoward, depends on which sort of defense can be offered, according to the (NA)*. Consequently, the (NA) cannot appeal to the relative untowardness of the S in question as one of the factors which makes a defense only meliorating as opposed to normatively exculpating.

The relation of the untowardness of S to what sort of defense can be offered is just the opposite of what the (NA) holds. *As a matter of fact, what sort of defense can be offered depends, in part, on the relative untowardness of S*. Consequently, we can treat neither meliorating nor normatively exculpating defenses as functioning by showing something about the untowardness of the relevant S. To properly analyze these defenses we must offer a (PA) theory.

The points made in this section strongly recommended the analyses I have offered, in as much as they are (PA) proposals. Hopefully, the examples considered strongly recommend the specific content of these proposals. However, I want to point out that these analyses are only partially complete. A full analysis would include a picture of the normative code which would render blaming someone for S unjustifiable, when S was produced in the presence of some (Nbr).[10]

---

[10] This picture would help us to place a particular plea in one or more of the types of defense we have considered. (Cf. Richard B. Brandt, *op. cit.*, p. 340.) If there are different normative codes to be considered, this placement might vary, even though the general analyses of different types of defenses given above would not vary. That is, whether a particular plea is a justification or a meliorating defense, for example, might vary with different codes while the general nature of defenses of these types remains the same. But we cannot discuss this further here.

Before offering some concluding remarks, a note on terminology might be in order. We set out to get a bit more understanding of "mitigating" and exculpating excuses. I have recommended our distinguishing between mitigating and meliorating defenses as well as between logically and normatively exculpating defenses. Have we distinguished four sorts of excuses? The only way to answer that question is to decide how we are going to speak. In much of the literature on excuses, normatively exculpating defenses are the primary object of investigation. In line with this, I would suggest that we reserve "excuse" for such defenses, and for meliorating defenses. Mitigating and logically exculpating defenses function so differently from the former, that clarity would be served by the usage I suggest.

6. CHARGES AND DEFENSES

A point raised earlier needs emphasizing. Against some charges, some defenses can be logically exculpating or mitigating and, against other charges, these defenses can be normatively exculpating or meliorating. The presence of the same circumstances which "get P off" in one way, relative to one charge, may do so in another way, relative to another charge. And, the same circumstances may get P off in any of the four ways we have considered, depending on the nature of the charge.

Consider the defense in the gun-injury case. The blame-relieving circumstance here is a mistake in judgment about the nature of the object. The presence of this circumstance could be logically exculpating in the face of the charge that P is blameworthy for giving a real gun to his child to play with, even though no harm was done. It could be mitigating, in the face of the charge that P is blameworthy for *deliberately* shooting and wounding another man. And we have seen that it can be meliorating or normatively exculpating in the face of the charge that P is blameworthy for shooting and wounding another.

Most, perhaps all, circumstances which "get P off" could do so in these four ways. How they did so would be a function, in part, of the charge being answered. We should remember this in investigating defenses.[11]

[11] I am indebted to Richard B. Brandt, William K. Frankena, and Jack W. Meiland for their helpful comments on earlier versions of this discussion.

University of Wyoming

Retributive Penal Liability

CLAUDIA CARD

I

AMONG the moral objections to punishment, two are outstanding: (1) punishment adds further suffering to the suffering caused by crime, and (2) in punishing the offender, we are sacrificing his well-being for the sake of that of others. The first objection is based upon a presumption against increasing human suffering; the second, upon a presumption of equality among persons in bearing communal burdens and sharing communal benefits. A plausible reply to the first objection is that punishment prevents more suffering than it causes. The deterrent theory takes this stand. The second objection is more difficult to answer. A retributive theory may attempt to meet this objection by arguing that punishment is a means by which the presumption of equality is maintained when some members of the community have failed to fulfill their obligations to others. The offender is held to deserve punishment from the others on the basis of his having taken an unfair advantage of their contributions to a common good.

The present essay offers such a retributive justification of liability to punishment. A principle of retributive penal liability is represented below as a companion to other principles of justice, and the relations between them are discussed. Briefly, the position to be developed is that the offender is not treated simply as a means to the good of others provided that he is made liable to punishment in return for his having culpably taken unfair advantage of them in his commission of an offense against just laws, when it is in the interests of everyone, including himself, to provide for such liability. The charge of inequality is met by the argument that, under a just system of punishment, everyone is able to avoid penal liability by his own reasonable choices, that the benefits arising from having the system are fairly made available to everyone who lives under it, and that penal liability can be made to serve as an equivalent substitute for the burden one is expected to bear, through obedience to just laws, in maintaining the common good. I am primarily concerned to develop the latter idea. Accordingly, punishment is represented better as a forfeiture than as a sacrifice.

17

The retributive view presented herein is not a comprehensive theory of punishment. It responds specifically to one objection, not to every objection that can be brought against the practice. However, that objection is not likely to be raised unless a tentative answer has been proposed in response to the first objection. It is important, then, to coordinate the retributive justification with a plausible response to the objection to making anyone suffer. The result is a coordination of retributive and deterrent justifications. However, neither is taken as fundamental to the other. In this way, the present account of retributive liability to punishment differs from most recent accounts.

Several recent attempts to reconcile justifications of punishment that have been traditionally set in opposition to each other (notably, those based upon considerations of retribution, deterrence, and reform) have consisted in trying to show that the different justifications should be seen as providing the bases of different kinds of decisions to be made about punishment. Examples are the decision whether to make certain sorts of conduct punishable, the decision whether to hold an individual liable to punishment, the decision how severely to punish, the decision what kind of punishment to impose, and so on. Curiously, it has been suggested that retributive justifications are peculiarly appropriate to the decisions of the judge, who has to apply the law to particular cases, while deterrent and reformative justifications are peculiarly appropriate to the decisions of the legislator, who designs the law. In its most nearly coherent form, this suggestion takes deterrent and reformative views as fundamental to a retributive view.[1] However, the idea of attempting to resolve conflicts between different sorts of grounds for punishing by means of a division of tasks seems superficial. For the problem is not who is to apply different criteria, but how the criteria are to be related to each other.

The value of looking at justifications of punishment from the point of view of the legislator is brought out by considering a model recently elaborated by John Rawls, according to which principles of social justice may be seen as

... principles which mutually self-interested and rational persons, when similarly situated and required to make in advance a firm commitment,

[1] On reconciling retributive with deterrent views, at least partly by a division of tasks between legislators and judges, see W. D. Ross, *The Right and the Good* (Oxford, 1930), pp. 61–64; J. D. Mabbott, "Punishment," *Mind*, vol. 48 (1939), pp. 152–167 and "Professor Flew on Punishment," *Philosophy*, vol. 30 (1955), pp. 256–265; John Rawls, "Two Concepts of Rules," *The Philosophical Review*, vol. 64 (1955), pp. 3–32; and S. I. Benn, "An Approach to the Problems of Punishment," *Philosophy*, vol. 33 (1958), pp. 325–341.

could acknowledge as restrictions governing the assignment of rights and duties in their common practices.[2]

Such persons may be regarded as ideal legislators. The ideal legislator can be expected to take into account the advantages and disadvantages of living under his decisions from the point of view of the representative person who would stand to gain the least, for the ideal legislator is required to make a "firm commitment in advance" of knowing how he, in particular, will be affected by his own decisions.

From this point of view, it becomes apparent that more than one kind of justification is relevant to many of the decisions to be made by the legislator with respect to punishment. The decision how severely to punish has, perhaps, proved most baffling on this account. There appear to be at least three competing criteria for determining the severity of punishment, which seem equally rational. One is the degree of the offender's culpability. A second is the harmfulness of the offense. And a third is the deterrent value of the threat of the penalty. The conflicts arising from applying these criteria are well-known, not only between retributive and deterrent points of view but also between different types of retributive theory. An offense causing little harm may be committed through a more serious fault than is another more harmful offense committed under extenuating circumstances. Here a conflict arises between the criteria of harm and culpability. By the criterion of harm, it seems the latter offense should be punished more severely than the former. By the criterion of culpability, the opposite seems true. The severity of the penalty required for deterrence may impose a greater hardship upon the offender than the offense itself could reasonably be expected to cause anyone. Here, there seems to be a conflict between the criteria of harm and deterrence. The criterion of harm seems to indicate a *less* severe penalty than is apparently needed for deterrence. Finally, a more severe penalty than is warranted by the harmfulness of the offense may be needed to deter persons precisely in circumstances which are extenuating with respect to culpability. In this case, each of the three criteria may call for a penalty different in severity from that indicated by each of the other two.

Is there any way out of this trilemma? Attempts have been made to subsume two of the criteria under the other and to show that there is one fundamental principle underlying all three, as when an adherent of the deterrent view appeals to the Principle of Utility. By and large, these attempts have demanded either an unwarranted optimism about

[2] "Justice as Fairness," *The Philosophical Review*, vol. 67 (1958), p. 174.

the facts of life—as when it is maintained that it would not be beneficial on the whole to punish offenses committed without fault—or else a willingness to abandon those convictions that gave rise to the problems in the first place, as when it is suggested that it may be right, after all, to execute psychotic offenders.[3] As an alternative to abandoning the problem and to searching for a common denominator, I propose to formulate the principle of retributive penal liability in such a way that it takes these criteria themselves as fundamental and gives an independent weight to each.

A first step out of the trilemma over the severity of punishment is to free the deterrent view from its long-standing association with Utilitarianism. Since Bentham, it has usually been taken for granted that a deterrent justification of punishment is only a consequence of applying the Principle of Utility. A deterrent justification is correctly acknowledged as utilitar*ian*, in the plain sense of an argument that the end justifies the means. Such a justification, however, does not imply Utilitarian*ism*, in the technical sense of a theory maintaining that the end sufficient to justify any means is "the greatest good of the greatest number" or "the greatest balance of happiness on the whole." The end sought may be, rather, "the *common* good," or, more specifically "a mutual assurance of general obedience to the law," and this end may be subject to various qualifications.

A helpful way of looking at punishment is to see it as capable of serving as a mutually acceptable stabilizer for cooperative enterprises. Cooperative undertakings intended to benefit all participants can be unstable in the following ways.[4] If less than universal cooperation is sufficient to obtain the benefits for all, it may be to anyone's advantage not to observe the rules when he thinks most others will observe them. Further, if he suspects that most others are not going to observe them, it may be foolish or dangerous for him to do so.[5] Since each can realize that everyone else may reason in the same way, everyone may

[3] See Jeremy Bentham, "Cases Unmeet for Punishment," *Principles of Morals and Legislation* (New York, 1948), chap. xiii. For the recommendation of capital punishment ("judicial homicide") for psychotic killers, see Jacques Barzun, "In Favor of Capital Punishment," *American Scholar*, vol. 31 (1962), pp. 182–191.

[4] For this way of presenting the instabilities to which cooperative schemes are subject, I am indebted to Rawls, "The Sense of Justice," *The Philosophical Review*, vol. 72 (1963), pp. 290–291. Rawls also suggests that the Hobbsian sovereign be viewed as a stabilizer. See W. D. Runciman and A. K. Sen, "Games, Justice and the General Will," *Mind*, vol. 74 (1965), pp. 554–562, for the idea that so stabilizing the common good gives an interpretation of Rousseau's claim that members of a community may be "forced to be free."

[5] Cf. Yossarian's response to Major Major [sic] in Joseph Heller's *Catch 22* (New York, 1961), chap. ix: "But suppose everybody on our side felt that way." "Then I'd certainly be a damned fool to feel any other way. Wouldn't I?"

become reluctant to cooperate. How is anyone to have confidence that most others will abide by the rules? Perhaps each will decline out of fear that his efforts would be wasted (or worse) because he sees that everyone else may think he will not cooperate, anyway, when he realizes that his efforts are not strictly needed and that they may think the same of everyone else as well. A penalty system might reduce the likelihood of its being to anyone's advantage not to observe the rules even when he thinks others will observe them and, thereby, reduce the first kind of suspicion directly, and, indirectly, the second as well.

Still, a penalty system might not be sufficient to eliminate instability if most participants neither were mutually bound by ties of friendship nor had—and were mutually aware of having—a sense of justice. The penalty system itself might then be subject to the same sorts of instability as the enterprise without penalties. Rawls has argued that "a system in which each person has, and is known by everyone to have, a sense of justice is inherently stable."[6] If we suppose, with Rawls, that everyone, or nearly everyone, is capable of a sense of justice, then perhaps the problem of instability is solved by developing that sense and achieving a mutual communication of it. A system of penalties might be made to serve that purpose. That is, a just system of penalties may help to promote a state of affairs in which everyone comes to realize that everyone else has a sense of justice. Suppose the community is democratic. The continued willingness of each to support a system under which he becomes liable to penalties in case of his failures to abide by the laws can be seen as a demonstration of his good faith to the others.

We need not suppose that a community can be suddenly formed out of a state of nature by everyone's agreeing to submit to a system of penalties. The same difficulties that give rise to instability in a cooperative system might present obstacles to such an agreement. We may suppose, rather, that penalty systems arise naturally—through theocracies and other authoritarian governments in political history and through parental discipline in that of the individual—and are gradually improved as persons come to recognize each other as equals (particularly in respect of their fallibility of judgment and moral weaknesses) and to appreciate the functions of penalties and their significance from the point of view of justice.[7] The ultimate goal of the penalty system might entail that the system itself would become superfluous. At least, the ideal underlying it seems to be a state of

[6] "The Sense of Justice," *op. cit.*, p. 293.
[7] Cf. Jean Piaget, *The Moral Judgment of the Child*, tr. by Marjorie Gabain (New York, 1932), chap. iii, sects. 1–4.

affairs in which the infliction of penalties is not really needed.[8] Thus, punishment is not taken as an end in itself.

When a cooperative enterprise has become a reasonably successful on-going concern and its regulations are tolerably just, mutual obligations arise on the part of its participants which cannot be accounted for satisfactorily independently of these facts. Failures to abide by the rules can deserve a kind of moral reprobation which would not be appropriate in a highly unstable arrangement. In such a context, penalties may be appropriately regarded as punishments. For they come to be expressive of the reprobation deserved by the offender from the others when he violates the mutual confidence that has arisen among them.[9] Where an imperfect system of penalties is already in operation, principles underlying just rules of liability may be taken to express fundamental ideas of the existing system and to serve as standards by reference to which it may be improved.

II

I offer the following principle as the basis of a retributive justification of punishment, underlying just rules of liability, and as a partial solution to the problem of conflicting criteria for determining severity. Penal deprivation of a person's general or special rights is not arbitrary if (1) he incurs liability to such deprivation only to the extent of his evident culpable failure to abide by a law of his community which is fairly designed to regulate conduct for the sake of the common good, (2) the hardship to which he is thus exposed in being made so liable does not exceed the worst that anyone could reasonably be expected to suffer from the similar conduct of another if such conduct were to become general in the community, and (3) provision for such liability can be expected to work to the advantage of everyone in maintaining a reasonable mutual assurance of general obedience to the law. The three divisions of the principle might naturally be regarded as three principles, since each appears to set out a fundamental limiting condition. However, these three conditions are offered, for the present, only as jointly sufficient to justify punishment

[8] For elaboration of the point that it is the awareness of provision for punishment, and not simply the infliction of punishment, which accounts for deterrence, see Mabbott, "Punishment," *op. cit.* Mabbott's view, like Bentham's, need supplementation by an appreciation of the sense of justice which both contributes to and qualifies the deterrent value of various kinds of "threats."

[9] See Joel Feinberg, "The Expressive Functions of Punishment," *Monist*, vol. 49 (1965), pp. 397–423, on distinguishing punishments from other penalties in terms of the moral significance of the former.

against the objection from equality. For convenience, I refer to the
entire set as the "Penalty Principle."

A basic idea of the Penalty Principle is that punishment is a just
return for failure to fulfill one's duty of fair play. Obligations to abide
by just laws of one's community may be seen as instances of this duty.
H. L. A. Hart has pointed out that political obligations cannot be
properly appreciated apart from what he has called a "mutuality of
restrictions." That is,

> ... when a number of persons conduct any joint enterprise according to
> rules and thus restrict their liberty, those who have submitted to these
> restrictions when required have a right to a similar submission from those
> who have benefited by their submission, . . . , the moral obligation to
> obey the rules in such circumstances is *due to* the co-operating members
> of the society.[10]

The kind of obligation to which Hart refers is identified by Rawls as
the *prima facie* duty of fair play. Rawls adds the qualification that the
enterprise be acknowledged to be fair, and he makes it explicit as part
of a set of sufficient conditions for incurring this obligation that one
has "knowingly participated in and accepted the benefits of" the
enterprise, without having lodged complaints against the rules prior
to the time at which it falls upon one to comply with them.[11] If we
accept Hart's understanding of "having a right against another" as
"having a moral justification for limiting the freedom of another,"
provision for liability to punishment may be seen as a morally justifiable limit placed upon the freedom of others by each member of the
community who has a right to their submission to its laws.

According to Hart, the acquired right correlative to the incurred
obligation to submit to the rules relies for its justification upon the
recognition of a certain natural right:

> ... any adult human being capable of choice (1) has the right to fore-
> bearance on the part of all others from the use of coercion or restraint
> against him save to hinder coercion or restraint and (2) is at liberty to do
> (i.e., is under no obligation to abstain from) any action which is not one
> coercing or restraining or designed to injure other persons.[12]

Hart calls this "the equal right of all men to be free." A basically
similar idea is found in the first of two principles presented by Rawls
as partially definitive of the justice of practices:

> ... first, each person participating in a practice, or affected by it, has an
> equal right to the most extensive liberty compatible with a like liberty for

[10] "Are There Any Natural Rights?" *The Philosophical Review*, vol. 64 (1955),
p. 185.
[11] "Justice as Fairness," *op. cit.*, pp. 179–180.
[12] *Ibid.*, p. 175.

all; and second, inequalities are arbitrary unless it is reasonable to expect that they will work out for everyone's advantage, and provided the positions and offices to which they attach, or from which they may be gained, are open to all.[13]

Either Hart's "equal right to be free" or Rawls's "greatest equal liberty principle" may be regarded as the source of the general rights referred to in the Penalty Principle.[14] The Penalty Principle may be seen at work in the qualifications upon rights and liberty given in Hart's statement of the equal right to be free. The "right to forebearance" might be secured by means of punishment if punishment meets the conditions of the Penalty Principle.

Rawls's second principle, to which he refers elsewhere[15] as "the difference principle," qualifies his first one by stating conditions under which inequalities are justifiable. The difference principle may be regarded as the source of the special rights referred to in the Penalty Principle. By the difference principle, we are prohibited from granting special rights to persons in some positions at the cost of a loss of well-being to persons in other positions. We are not allowed to defeat the presumption of equal liberty by the argument permitted by Classical Utilitarianism that the losses to some persons are outweighed by the gains to others. Similarly, by the Penalty Principle, we are not allowed to justify a penal deprivation of a person's rights by the argument that the offender's losses are outweighed by the gains to others who benefit by the example. Provision for liability to punishment is justifiable, rather, in terms of advantages thereby secured for everyone, including the offender, contingently upon his own choices. The loss with which anyone is threatened by punishment must be outweighed by advantages made available *to him* through general obedience to the law and must not outweigh the disadvantages anyone could reasonably be expected to suffer from another were there no such general cooperation. It is not that the consequences of one's decisions to obey the law must in every case be preferable to the consequences of deciding to disobey. The advantages made available by general cooperation are not a consequence of one's decisions in this manner. One can be expected already to have enjoyed such advantages prior to the time at which it falls upon one to make such a decision. The Penalty Principle allows the continued enjoyment of

<hr />

[13] *Ibid.*, p. 165.

[14] See Hart's discussion of "general rights" as exemplifications of the equal right to be free, *op. cit.*, pp. 187–188.

[15] "Distributive Justice" in *Philosophy Politics and Society* (3d Series), ed. by Peter Laslett and W. D. Runciman (Oxford, 1967).

(some) such advantages to be contingent upon one's fulfillment of the duty of fair play.

Neither the difference principle nor the Penalty Principle entirely defeats the initial presumption of equal freedom. By the difference principle, a fair opportunity is allowed to substitute for an equal right, where the advantages in question cannot be granted to everyone. By the Penalty Principle, a fair opportunity to avoid becoming an offender through one's own reasonable choices is intended as a condition of the justice of punishment. Whether this fair opportunity exists depends greatly upon the justice of the laws of the community, apart from punishment. As T. H. Green has put the matter,

> . . . the justice of the punishment depends on the justice of the general system of rights; not merely on the propriety with reference to social well-being of maintaining this or that particular right which the crime punished violates, but on the question whether the social organisation in which a criminal has lived and acted is one that has given him a fair chance of not being a criminal.[16]

The fair opportunity also depends, however, upon the rules of liability of the institution of punishment itself. In discussing the "openness" of positions referred to in the difference principle, Rawls is not specific about the nature of the relevant merits on which persons are to be judged in fair competition for such positions. The Penalty Principle, however, is specific about the nature of penal desert. The condition of evident culpable failure is intended not to allow punishment for violations which the offender could not fairly have been expected to avoid committing. Both the first and second divisions of the Penalty Principle point toward further specifications of penal desert in terms of degrees of culpability and of the harmfulness of the offense.

The condition that provision for penal liability be to everyone's advantage in maintaining a reasonable mutual assurance of general obedience to just laws is roughly analogous to the requirement of the difference principle that everyone be better off as the result of allowing inequalities. Again, however, the Penalty Principle is specific about the nature of the justifying advantage. It is to be expected that in designing penalties no more severe deprivation will be permitted than *the least that is sufficient* to maintain a reasonable mutual assurance of general obedience on the part of persons who might otherwise be suspected of the same fault as the offender. This qualification accords with the spirit of Rawls's first principle, which gives "the most extensive liberty compatible with a like liberty for all," rather than

---

[16] *Lectures on the Principles of Political Obligation* (London, 1941), p. 186.

C

simply "an equal liberty for each." Since no one can be entirely confident that he will not be convicted in error or that he will not succumb to temptation or yield to the pressure of circumstances and disobey when he could still obey, each will find it reasonable to have provision for the *least* severe penalty sufficient to assure general obedience under the various circumstances in which the temptation to disobey may arise. The desirable generality of obedience may vary with the harmfulness of the offense. And the harmfulness of some offenses will vary with the prevalence of temptation to commit them. Thus, the least severe penalty sufficient to give a reasonable assurance of general obedience may not be determinable without a good deal of empirical data.

The following disanalogies between the difference principle and the Penalty Principle should be apparent. First, the difference principle is intended to justify exceptional social positions in the basic structure of a community or practice, while the Penalty Principle is intended, rather, to allow qualifications upon everyone's rights. Ideally, no one would ever be in the position of an offender. Second, liability to a penalty is intended as a consequence of one's own choices, whereas qualification for special rights need not be interpreted, even ideally, as a consequence of one's own choices. Justice in punishment does not involve competition, and it is supposed that everyone can avoid liability to punishment.

When the conditions of the Penalty Principle are satisfied for a given case, the offender's liability to punishment is justified against the charge of inequality. He cannot complain that he is being made to contribute more to the well-being of others than they have contributed to his own well-being. Thus, he has no complaint on grounds of his rights against his being made to suffer in order to maintain benefits in which he may no longer have a share, or in which his share is significantly reduced. Further complaints against inflicting the penalty must appeal to something other than his rights, as when a plea for mercy is entered.

III

The retributive core of the Penalty Principle stands in most obvious need of elucidation and interpretation. The problems presented for interpreting and applying the culpability and deterrent conditions are no less difficult than those presented for the condition of harm. In what follows, however, I do not take up the special problems involved in understanding culpability and deterrence but simply attempt to clarify the condition of harm and indicate its relationship to the other conditions of the Penalty Principle. An understanding of this retributive core of the principle is crucial to clearing up some apparent conflicts between the criteria of harm, deterrence, and culpability in determining the severity of punishment. For it gives an interpretation of the relevance of harm allowing that there can be retributive grounds for making an offender liable to suffer more or less than he caused anyone to suffer by his offense. Considerations of culpability and deterrence may place further qualifications upon the severity of his punishment. But it is important to realize that an appeal to such factors need not alter the retributive status of a punishment which causes greater or less suffering to the offender than he caused anyone by his offense.

In interpreting the Penalty Principle, I understand "persons" as "human beings who are legal persons." I have not attempted to extend the ideas of the principle to corporate bodies which are also considered legal persons, primarily because "suffering" and "fault" seem to have only a metaphorical application to corporate bodies (although such bodies can be granted and deprived of rights and can incur obligations, in some sense). However, I have not meant to exclude human beings who are members of corporate bodies.

When the culpability and deterrent conditions of the first and third divisions of the Penalty Principle do not call for a less severe penalty, the principle establishes a presumption in favor of liability to what I call the *Full Measure* of punishment. The Full Measure consists in a deprivation of rights exposing the offender to a hardship comparable in severity to the worst that anyone could reasonably be expected to suffer from the similar conduct of another if such conduct were to become general in the community—but no greater deprivation than that. The relevant hardship for comparison is that which one individual would suffer from another in the context of general conduct similar to the offense. It is not intended that we total the hardships inflicted by an offender upon all or several persons and inflict a comparable hardship (if the idea makes sense) upon him. Nor is it intended that we total the hardships inflicted by several offenders upon someone and inflict anything comparable upon one offender. The Full Measure of punishment also differs from the usual interpretations of "an eye for an eye" in that it is not intended primarily to indicate the *kind* of penalty or the nature of the hardship to be suffered by the offender, but, rather, the *severity* of the penalty. Other considerations than severity are relevant to evaluating kinds of punishment, not the least of which is revocability or reparability in case of a wrong conviction.[17] The reciprocity suggested by the Penalty Principle does suggest, however, that one think in terms of rights of which the offender might fairly be deprived.

The most troublesome ideas in the Full Measure of punishment are the "generalization provision" and the specification of "the *worst* that anyone might reasonably be expected to suffer." Since it is easier to deal with the latter specification after having explained the generalization provision, I take up that provision first. Why is it there? (Why not say, simply, "the hardship anyone might reasonably be expected to suffer from another who acted likewise"?) How general are we to hypothesize the indulgence in this sort of conduct in order to determine the Full Measure? (Are we to imagine *everyone* in the community committing the same offense? is that possible? or, just most members? or many members? if so, how many?) And, what are we supposed to be generalizing? action having certain harmful results? creating a certain danger? or something else?

The reason for having a generalization provision, in the first place, is that many offenses fail to cause any real harm, or much real harm, only because most persons are abiding by the law which the offender violated. In such cases, it may be no credit to the offender that he did not hurt anyone very much. That credit may be due to the cooperating members of the community whose conduct makes it a real possibility for some to disobey without disastrous consequences. If others who were similarly tempted to act as the offender had succumbed to the temptation, the harm likely to result from the conduct of any of them might have been far greater. Thus, one cannot claim the fact that no one was hurt by the offense as indicative of the seriousness of that offense, from the point of view of justice, when that fact is traceable to the submission of others to the law violated by the offender.

For example, if many persons were to forge signatures on checks, one who receives checks may receive a number of bad ones. While one bad check by itself may not cause much harm, the same bad check received as one of several may be a far greater loss. First, it may be greater because the same amount of money can have a greater value when one has not much money altogether. Second, it could be a contributing factor to a general breakdown of the check-credit system. This is not to identify the relevant hardship with the

[17] See Bentham, *op. cit.*, chap. xi for evaluations of kinds of penalties carried out largely independently of the issue of severity. Contrast Kant, *Metaphysical Elements of Justice: Part I of the Metaphysics of Morals*, tr. by John Ladd (Indianapolis, 1965), pp. 101–102, on the *lex talionis* as the criterion of the just kind and degree of punishment. See, also, Piaget, *loc. cit.*, for a more sophisticated conception of reciprocity in kind.

total hypothetical loss from bad checks, but, rather, to call attention to the difference in hardship caused to anyone by one such offense committed in the context of general obedience to the relevant laws and committed in the opposite context of widespread disregard of such laws.[18]

It may be objected, however, that ordinarily everyone knows that general breakdowns of entire systems, such as check-credit systems or traffic systems, are not going to be brought about. It is altogether unrealistic to suppose that one offense could set such a powerful example. Most people want to follow the rules most of the time. Just how general is the extent of disobedience in the context of which it is reasonable to place a given offense? If we take it that the present offense is already contributing to such general breakdowns, why not say that every offense committed, no matter what it is, is contributing to a general breakdown of law and order? The likely consequence of that, for anyone, is a life that is "solitary, poor, nasty, brutish, and short." So why not say simply that the Full Measure of punishment for every offense is death or banishment? Were that its implication, the second division of the Penalty Principle would seem superfluous for the purpose of grading the punishments in severity.

In responding to this objection, it is important, first, to realize that the point of referring to general similar conduct is *not* that a given offense is actually contributing to any such eventuality, and, second, to consider why a general breakdown of law and order is not going to occur. It seems reasonable to place a given offense in the context of conduct of a certain sort only when it is reasonable to believe that there *would be* a real likelihood of general conduct of that sort were there no law making such conduct an offense. We may, then, regard some offenses as contributing hypothetically to a disaster, but it is crucial to bear in mind the hypothesis. Those who would not engage in such conduct even without the law are not taken into account in projecting "what would happen if everyone did that."[19] Persons who have no occasion to commit the offense, are not tempted to do it, or have some special interest in not doing it, apart from its being a violation of

---

[18] I am indebted to Norman Gillespie for pointing out to me the importance, from the standpoint of fairness, of distinguishing between the harm likely to result to anyone *from general disobedience* and the harm likely to result to anyone *from the disobedience of another in the context of general disobedience.*

[19] On differences between the generalization argument in ethics and indirect utilitarianism, see Marcus G. Singer, *Generalization in Ethics* (New York, 1961), chap. vii, sect. 4. The element of fairness involved in restricting "relevantly similar persons" to "everyone who wants to do likewise" was made clear to me by Norman Gillespie in "Fundamental Moral Principles," unpublished Ph.D. Dissertation, University of Wisconsin, Madison, Wisconsin, 1970.

the law, are not taken advantage of unfairly by offenders as are those who would be tempted but have refrained because of the law. If most persons would not even be tempted to engage in some sort of conduct and the few who would do so would cause no harm thereby, it would be unreasonable to make that conduct punishable. Of course, some offenses, such as murder, are harmful enough in themselves that the generalization provision is superfluous. The sort of conduct for which that provision is designed is that which is likely to produce harm, or a significantly greater harm, only when a number of persons engage in it. The answer to the question, "how general?" is "only general enough to include those who are tempted to engage in similar conduct or have some interest in doing so and those who would be so tempted or would have such an interest, were the conduct in question not prohibited by law."

Ordinarily, I would suppose, even if the number of persons who would be tempted to forge checks were sufficient to endanger the entire check-credit system, a total breakdown of law and order would not thereby become a realistic hypothesis. Only in a state of extreme emergency would it seem justifiable to regard almost any form of disobedience as realistically contributing to a hypothetical breakdown of law and order. Perhaps such a rationale partially underlies the severity of military discipline.

It may be objected, further, however, that it is not sufficiently clear how we are to understand "similar conduct." Everyone who is tempted to commit any offense is tempted to engage in conduct similar to that of anyone else who commits any offense whatever, namely, conduct which is in violation of the law. If the Full Measure of punishment is interpreted that loosely, it will be impossible, again, to make the intended distinctions between the harmfulness of different offenses.

The easiest way to specify relevant similarity is to say "the same kind of offense as specified by the law." One reason the principle is not stated in this way is to preclude distinguishing some offenses from others as mere "attempts" where the attempt has failed owing entirely to circumstances not reasonably foreseeable. The hardship one could reasonably be expected to suffer from any such attempt is no different from that which one could reasonably be expected to suffer from a successful attempt. By hypothesis, the failure of the attempt was not reasonably foreseeable. Thus, an attempt to murder, in which it is evident that the agent has taken the last step (say, aimed his loaded gun properly and pulled the trigger), and which fails owing entirely to unforeseeable circumstances (say, the intended victim moves, or drops dead of a heart attack) is not to be regarded as conduct relevantly different from (successful) murder.[20] Likewise, an offense is not bo be distinguished as one of a different kind only by the fact that it led accidentally to disastrous consequences which were not reasonably foreseeable. The "reasonable expectation" is to be understood from the point of view of the agent, although on the hypothesis that others were to act likewise, where their doing so would increase the harm likely to result from any individual offense. An assault accidentally causing death, then, when the accident was not reasonably foreseeable, is not to be distinguished for purposes of punishment from a plain assault, although it may call for special consideration in terms of compensation to the victim's family. The question "what should be allowed to count as an offense?" cannot be settled simply in terms of harm. The point can be made that unforeseeable accidental consequences and failures ought not to be taken as criteria distinguishing one kind of offense from another. In this respect, they are on a par with the absence of harmful consequences owing to the obedience of others to the law violated by the offender. The offender does not deserve credit for any of them.

In figuring the hardship one could be expected to suffer from the offense, it seems fair to anticipate the *worst likely* hardship that would result, foreseeably, *to anyone*, either from the offense alone or from such an offense committed in the context of general similar conduct. It is not intended that we simply estimate the likelihood of anyone's being victimized in a certain way by the offense, even with the generalization provision. It may be likely that someone or other would suffer severely and yet not very likely that any given member of the community would be the one to suffer. Or, it may be that the average likelihood of one's becoming the victim is low, although the likelihood for persons in some circumstances is high. Failing to provide protection for a minority who can be expected to need it greatly would be sacrificing their safety for the sake of convenience to the rest. On a Classical Utilitarian calculation, the sum of conveniences to a majority might outweigh the sum of dangers to a minority. From the point of view of justice, however, we need only consider whether the convenience to the individual who would be least well off would outweigh the danger risked by him.

It may appear that taking the point of view of those likely to suffer

[20] Attempts in which the last step has not been taken are relevantly different from this sort of case. For a helpful discussion of the significance of requiring external conduct for a criminal offense, see Herbert Morris, "Punishment for Thoughts," *Monist*, vol. 49 (1965), pp. 342–376.

worst is incompatible with, for example, regarding an assault which accidentally produces fatal consequences differently from an assault with intent to kill. For the sheer multiplicity of ordinary assaults seems to render it probable that someone will suffer a resulting fatal accident. The harm predictable in case of a large number of offenses of a certain sort may be great, though the harm foreseeable from any one of them remains small. So, why not take the *average* harm, instead of the *worst*?[21]

Since an accidental death by assault would clearly be the result of that assault only, it would seem unfair to hold other offenders even partially responsible for it. The circumstances giving rise to such accidents, such as a given victim's having a bad heart, are not—presumably—created by the multiplicity of offenses. The agent, then, would not be in a position to foresee the likelihood of such an accident, even on the hypothesis of general similar conduct, even though we can predict, statistically, that some number of victims are likely to be in the relevantly dangerous circumstances. Since this is not the sort of offense the harmfulness of which would be aggravated by the similar conduct of others, it would be unfair to take even the average harm predicted in such a manner as relevant to determining the severity of punishment. Figuring the likelihood of an accident by statistical predictability would be analogous to allowing a simple estimation of the likelihood of one's becoming the victim of an offense. A straight utilitarian calculation would, apparently, allow both; from the standpoint of justice, neither is legitimate.

IV

Ideally, the Full Measure of punishment would consist in a suspension or withdrawal of rights of the offender corresponding to his failure to respect such rights of others. This idea is also put forward by Ross:

> We do not see any *direct* moral relation to exist between wrong-doing and suffering so that we may say directly, such and such an offense deserves so much suffering, neither more nor less. But we do think that the injury to be inflicted on the offender should be *not much greater* [italics mine] than that which he has inflicted on another. Ideally, from this point of view, it should be no greater. For he has lost his *prima facie* rights to life, liberty, or property, only in so far as these rested on an explicit or implicit undertaking to respect the corresponding rights in others, and in so far as he has failed to respect those rights.[22]

[21] This objection was pointed out to me by Roderick Firth.
[22] *Op. cit.*, p. 62.

Ross's difficulty with relating the hardship deserved by an offender to the injury caused by his offense could be solved by considering not simply the hardship that actually results to the victim of the offense, but that which could reasonably be expected to result to someone if such conduct were indulged in generally by those who would have an interest in doing so. Thus, in a particular case, the deserved penalty may impose a greater or lesser hardship on the offender than was suffered by any victim of his offense.

Ross, however, seems to feel that considerations of the general interest would sometimes appropriately *increase* the severity of a penalty beyond that which is deserved by the offender:

> At the same time we recognize that this, while a *prima facie* duty, is not the only *prima facie* duty of the legislator; and that ... he must consider expediency, and may make the penalty more or less severe as it dictates. His action should, in fact, be guided by regard to the *prima facie* duty of injuring wrong-doers only to the extent that they have injured others, and also to the *prima facie* duty of promoting the general interest.[23]

By expediency in promoting the general interest, Ross probably has in mind the deterrent value of the threat of the penalty. Since he does not rank *prima facie* duties in a general way, he leaves us to our intuitions for determining which to weigh more heavily in a given kind of case: the need for protection against the commission of offenses of that kind? or, the desert of the offender? His conclusion is a compromise with no rationale. He seems to feel driven to admit that consideration of the general interest may call for a more severe penalty than is deserved. But, not liking this much, he tempers this judgment by saying the penalty should be "not much greater." Thus, he refuses to face up to the problem presented by a kind of offense that cannot be prevented except by a penalty much more severe than would be deserved.

The Penalty Principle avoids these difficulties in two ways. First, it interprets desert partly in terms of what is reasonable to expect would be suffered by someone if the offense were committed generally, and not simply in terms of what is actually (or even likely to be) suffered by the victim of an isolated offense. Second, it refuses to allow either considerations of deterrence to outweigh retributive ones, or vice versa. No penalty greater than the Full Measure is allowed for any offense, nor is any penalty allowed the threat of which would be more than sufficient to maintain a reasonable mutual assurance of general obedience to the law in circumstances similar to those of the offender.

The restriction on severity given by the Full Measure, then, presents

[23] *Ibid.*, pp. 62–63.

a major modification of Bentham's recommendation that the cost of prevention not exceed the mischief of the offense.[24] On Bentham's view, the cost is figured in terms of total suffering by all punished offenders, plus the total efforts and anxieties involved in enforcing the law, and weighed against the total suffering that would result otherwise to victims of the offense. By the Penalty Principle, the cost is figured from the standpoint of an individual member of the community who would be expected to offer support to the system and would become liable to punishment in case he committed the offense, or might otherwise become the least fortunate victim of the offense.

In practice, it is likely that a penalty more severe than the Full Measure will be proposed to compensate for uncertainty in the infliction of the penalty when the offense is difficult to detect, or when the offender is difficult to apprehend or convict, or when the commission of one offense facilitates the commission of still others. Thus, the death penalty, which would normally exceed the Full Measure, has been provided for rape and for kidnap, even though any murder or attempted murder involved could be treated as a separate offense. Offenses committed while the offender is armed with a dangerous weapon are often treated more severely than one would expect if the original offense, the danger presented by possession of the weapon, and any attempt to inflict injury with the weapon were treated separately. The category of "felony murder" is notoriously unjust when it includes the unforeseeable causing of accidental death.

When difficulties of detection, apprehension, or conviction make it likely that a sizable proportion of those who commit an offense will not be brought to justice, there arises the temptation to boost the deterrent value of the threat of punishment by increasing the severity of the penalty. Even if the penalty succeeds as a greater deterrent, if it exceeds the Full Measure, those who suffer it are made to pay *not only for their own offenses, but also, in part, for the offenses of others* who were clever enough or lucky enough not to be convicted. Deterrence so obtained reduces the incidence of offenses in an unfair way. For the offender is made to bear more than his fair share of the burden of maintaining the common good. While it may be more expedient to punish more severely than the Full Measure, there would be more justice in seeking a remedy for the conditions that make infliction of the penalty so highly uncertain.

The Full Measure thus qualifies the ways in which deterrence may justly be obtained by punishment. In other situations, the temptation arises to punish more severely than would be sufficient to maintain a

[24] Bentham, *op. cit.*, chap. xiii, sects. 1 and 4.

reasonable mutual assurance of general obedience. A murderer may deserve death; but, it is doubtful, at best, that a less severe penalty would not ordinarily be sufficient. The offender's desert is determined by his being at fault in failing to fulfill his duty of fair play, and the seriousness of his fault may be gauged partly (but only partly) by the foreseeable harm of such failures. It is only with this latter aspect of penal desert that the Full Measure deals. A fuller treatment would also consider the depth of the offender's breach of faith with members of the community and would show how this factor qualifies the severity of punishment indicated by the factors of harm and deterrence.

The objection from equality—that in punishing an offender, we are sacrificing his well-being for the sake of that of others—suggests that others have more to gain from the punishment of an offender than he has received from them. If the Penalty Principle were observed as I have interpreted it, this would not be true. The deprivation of rights to which an offender would be liable by that principle would expose him to a forfeiture of advantages no greater than those made available to him by the submission of others to the laws he failed to observe. If punishing him helps to maintain such advantages for others, it does for them only what his own obedience would have done. If he owes them such support, he can be made justly to provide it in one form or another.

University of Wisconsin, Madison

Is Mill's Hedonism Inconsistent?

NORMAN O. DAHL*

HEDONISM is that theory of value according to which pleasure and only pleasure is good. However, any adequate theory of value must provide not only a basis for judging whether an object or state of affairs is good or not, but also a basis for judging the comparative value of two objects or states of affairs. That is, it must provide a basis for judging whether or not one object or state of affairs is *better* than another. It is this aspect of hedonism that will occupy my attention in this paper, and it will be my general concern to consider what limitations there are within which any hedonistic theory of value must operate, in particular, whether a hedonistic theory of comparative value is committed to taking quantitative differences in pleasure as the only basis for determining the relative value of objects. I shall pursue this concern by considering the charge that has frequently been levelled at John Stuart Mill, that his brands of "qualitative" hedonism is inconsistent. It will be the purpose of this paper to show that this charge is unfounded, that there is nothing inconsistent about qualitative hedonism.

The paper is divided into six sections. In the first section I briefly spell out Mill's brand of hedonism and the considerations which prompted him to propose it. I also indicate the traditional response that has greeted Mill's proposal. Part of the purpose of this section is to indicate why the question of the consistency of qualitative hedonism is important. In the second section I set out what I take to be plausible candidates for conditions that any hedonistic theory of comparative value must meet. I do this first of all to provide a fairly clear and precise way of formulating the problem I am concerned with in this paper, and secondly to provide some basis for assessing the objections that have been raised against Mill. In the third section I consider arguments against the consistency of Mill's position that are based on his particular way of formulating qualitative hedonism, and I argue

* This paper grew in part out of a series of discussions with Gareth Matthews, and I am indebted to him for his suggestions. Earlier versions of it were read at St. Olaf College, the University of Minnesota and the Pacific Division meetings of the American Philosophical Association in March 1971. I have also benefitted from the comments of my colleagues William H. Hanson and Rolf E. Sartorius and from those of George E. Arbaugh.

that they do not show that Mill is inconsistent. In the final three sections I consider three arguments which, if they were sound, would show that any form of qualitative hedonism is inconsistent, and I indicate where they break down. The result of all of this, I think, will be that one will recognize that qualitative hedonism is a consistent theory of value.

I

Perhaps the best known hedonistic theory of comparative value is Jeremy Bentham's "hedonic calculus." According to Bentham there are six different dimensions within which pleasures may vary, differences within which determine their relative value,—intensity, duration, certainty or uncertainty (their likelihood of being experienced), remoteness or propinquity (length of time it would take to experience them), fecundity or purity (their tendency to be followed by further pleasure or pain), and extent (number of people experiencing the pleasure). All of these dimensions except those of certainty-uncertainty and remoteness-propinquity provide ways of determining the *quantity* of pleasure associated with a given object,[1] and for my purposes I think the dimensions of certainty-uncertainty and remoteness-propinquity can be disregarded.[2]

Bentham's "hedonic calculus" has been the target of a number of criticisms, but perhaps the best known of these is that it is open to some obvious counterexamples. There are cases in which an activity may produce as much or a greater amount of pleasure than some other activity, but nevertheless no one (except perhaps Bentham) would say that the first activity is better than the second. If, for example, playing pushpin gives a person as long and as intense pleasures as listening to poetry, then on Bentham's theory, pushpin is as good as poetry. Or, if a foolish person, because of his severely limited goals and desires, is able to satisfy a great number of desires and suffer little frustration, then his life will have to be judged better than that of someone like Socrates, who, because of the breadth and nature of his concerns, is bound to suffer a good deal of frustration. In short, Bentham is committed to the consequences that pushpin may be as good as poetry

---

[1] There is a genuine question, I think, over whether intensity of pleasure is a qualitative rather than a quantitative difference of pleasure, but I shall simply assume here that it is a quantitative difference.

[2] These dimensions are only relevant for determining the amount of pleasure one can *reasonably expect*; they have no bearing on the amount of pleasure that actually will be produced. If one assumes ideal conditions of knowledge, then considerations of certainty-uncertainty and remoteness-propinquity would play no role in determining the actual amount of pleasure produced by a given object.

and that a fool satisfied is better off than a Socrates dissatisfied. These consequences have struck a good many philosophers as simply mistaken.

It was in an attempt to avoid consequences such as these that Mill put forward his "qualitative" hedonism. In Chapter II of *Utilitarianism* Mill affirms a general hedonistic theory of value by saying,

> . . . pleasure, and freedom from pain, are the only things desirable as ends; and that all desirable things . . . are desirable either for the pleasure inherent in themselves, or as means to the promotion of pleasure and the prevention of pain.[3]

In answer to objections similar to those outlined above Mill replies,

> It is quite compatible with the principle of utility to recognize the fact, that some *kinds* of pleasure are more desirable and more valuable than others. It would be absurd that while in estimating all other things quality is considered as well as quantity, the estimation of pleasures should be supposed to depend on quantity alone.[4]

If there are qualitative differences in pleasure that bear on the relative value of different pleasures, then even though an activity like pushpin may produce pleasures equal to or greater in *amount* than those derived from listening to poetry, the *quality* of pleasure derived from listening to poetry may be high enough to outweigh the quantity of pleasure derived from pushpin. Similarly, though a fool may experience a greater quantity of pleasure throughout his lifetime than someone like Socrates, the pleasures of a Socrates may be of such a high quality that they will more than balance the greater amount of pleasure derived by the fool. It will then be open to the hedonist to conclude, as Mill does, "It is better to be a human dissatisfied than a pig satisfied; better to be a Socrates dissatisfied than a fool satisfied."[5]

The traditional response to Mill's attempt to avoid the sorts of objections we have been considering is that even though it allows Mill to avoid them, it does so at too great a cost. The view Mill is left with is inconsistent. He must either abandon the view that the quality of two different pleasures may determine their relative value, and so leave himself open to the objections that have been raised against Bentham, or he must give up hedonism. He cannot have it both ways. As A. C. Ewing put it,

> Mill tried indeed to reconcile his utilitatianism with the admission that a lesser pleasure might rationally be preferred to a greater on the grounds

---

[3] *Utilitarianism* (New York, 1957), pp. 10–11.
[4] *Ibid.*, p. 12.
[5] *Ibid.*, p. 4.

of the superior quality of the former, but it is generally, and I think rightly, agreed among philosophers that he failed to escape inconsistency.[6]

In the *Encyclopedia of Philosophy* Raziel Abelson says,

> But like Epicurus' preference to "natural" over "unnatural" pleasures, Mill's criterion of quality introduces a standard of value other than pleasure, by which pleasure itself can be evaluated, and thus contradicts the principle of utility, that pleasure is the single standard of good.[7]

Richard Taylor echoes the same criticism when he says

> The claim is just incoherent . . . if pleasure is the only thing good for its own sake and is the standard by which other things are deemed good, as hedonism declares, then no pleasure can be inherently better than others. Pleasures can in this case only differ in quantity . . . they cannot differ in their quality of goodness.[8]

I should point out that although this view about Mill's qualitative hedonism is widespread, it is by no means universal. William Frankena claims that the charge of inconsistency by critics of Mill is due to their identifying hedonism with quantitative hedonism.[9] Although I am in agreement with Professor Frankena, he does not go on to say why the arguments critics have given or might give for this identification are mistaken. This is something that should be done, and I shall try to do it in the latter parts of this paper. Ernest Sosa also argues that Mill is not inconsistent, but his argument is that Mill never did give up the view that the greater the pleasure the better it is.[10] In this it seems to me that Professor Sosa is mistaken, but rather than pursue this any further in this paper, what I shall do is argue that if Mill had given up the view that the greater pleasure is always the better, he would not have been inconsistent.

---

[6] *Ethics* (New York, 1965), p. 42.

[7] "History of Ethics," *The Encyclopedia of Philosophy*, vol. 3, ed. by Paul Edwards (New York, 1967), p. 97.

[8] *Good and Evil* (New York, 1970), p. 94. Others who more or less endorse the charge of inconsistency against Mill include Phillip Wheelwright, *A Critical Introduction to Ethics* (New York, 1959), pp. 58–59; John Hospers, *Human Conduct* (New York, 1961), p. 59; Richard Garner and Bernard Rosen, *Moral Philosophy* (New York, 1967), pp. 146 and 153; F. H. Bradley, "Pleasure For Pleasure's Sake," reprinted in *Mill's Utilitarianism*, ed. by James M. Smith and Ernest Sosa (Belmont, Calif., 1969), pp. 133–143; and G. E. Moore, *Principia Ethica* (Cambridge, 1954), pp. 77–81.

[9] *Ethics* (Englewood Cliffs, 1963), p. 69.

[10] "Mill's *Utilitarianism*" in *Mill's Utilitarianism*, *op. cit.*, pp. 154–172. See esp. pp. 161–172. In his comments on the version of this paper read at the Pacific Division APA meetings Professor Terence Penelhum also offered an interpretation of Mill according to which he is consistent but does not give up the view that always the greater the amount of pleasure the better.

I hope the importance of the question of the consistency of qualitative hedonism is obvious from what I have just said. If qualitative Hedonism will present a more vulnerable target to its critics if qualitawhich it would not be open if qualitative hedonism were consistent, namely those of the sort that were raised against Bentham's theory. Hedonism, will present a more vulnerable target to its critics if qualitative hedonism is inconsistent than it will if qualitative hedonism is not inconsistent.

II

In this section I shall set out what I take to be plausible candidates for conditions that any hedonistic theory of comparative value must meet. I do this in the first place to provide a tentative characterization of hedonism that does not beg the question I am interested in, secondly to provide a way of stating the main problem of this paper in a clearer and more precise way than has been done up to now, and finally to provide some basis for deciding whether the charge of inconsistency that has been leveled against Mill is correct or not.

There are two, possibly three, general conditions which, at least at the outset, any hedonistic theory of comparative value would be expected to fulfill. The first, of course, is that pleasure and only pleasure is good. The second is that any difference in value must be due to a difference in pleasure. This condition seems to follow from the first condition. Suppose two objects differed in value but there was no difference in the pleasures associated with them. Then there would have to be some difference between the objects, quite apart from the pleasures associated with them, that accounts for their difference in value. One of the objects would have to have, or have more of, a certain characteristic which the other lacked, or had less of, a characteristic other than that of being pleasant and one which had no bearing on the pleasantness of the objects. The possession of this characteristic, or of a certain degree of it, would have to be valuable in order to account for the difference in value between the two objects. From this it would seem to follow, however, that something quite different from and unrelated to pleasure was valuable, and therefore that hedonism was false. Thus, any hedonistic theory of comparative value must hold that differences in value are due to differences in pleasure.

To this second condition one may want to add a third, that one object is better than another if and only if (all things considered) it is more pleasant than the other. One reason for accepting this condition is as follows. To say that one object is better than another is simply to

D

say that it is more valuable than the other. Since according to hedonism, pleasure and only pleasure is valuable, one object will be better than another if and only if it is more pleasant than the other. That is, since what is valuable is what is pleasant and what is pleasant is what is valuable, what is more valuable should be what is more pleasant and vice versa. Therefore, one object will be better than another if and only if (all things considered) it is more pleasant.

At first sight this condition may seem to say no more than the second, but on reflection one can see that there are two reasons for distinguishing it from the second. In fact there are grounds for breaking it down into two additional conditions. The first thing this condition does is to limit the sorts of differences of pleasure that can make a difference to value. Consider a characteristic that admits of more or less, e.g., the characteristic of being charitable. We do sometimes say that one person is more charitable than another. Consider now the sorts of differences that might hold between the "charitableness" of two different people. There are differences between the charitableness of two people which provide grounds for saying that one of the two is more charitable than the other, and there are differences which provide no such grounds. For example, if the charitableness of Jones differs from that of Smith in that it involves a greater percentage of Jones's income than does Smith's, one would have grounds for saying that Jones is more charitable than Smith. However, Jones's charitableness may also differ from Smith's in that it is directed primarily towards helping children while Smith's charitableness is not restricted in this way. This difference would provide no grounds for saying that Jones is more or less charitable than Smith. This example illustrates that there are some characteristics that admit of two kinds of differences, one which bears on whether something has more or less of that characteristic and the other of which does not. The third condition stated above adds to the second condition the requirement that the differences between pleasures that determine differences in value must be differences that also determine whether something is more or less pleasant. The second thing this condition adds is that comparative value is always directly proportional to pleasure, i.e., it is always the case that the more pleasant the better. If one only accepted the first two conditions, it would be possible to hold a hedonistic theory of value according to which the less pleasure the better, and this would be strange, to say the least.

What I am concerned with in this paper, then, are theories of comparative value that satisfy at least the first two and possibly also the third of the following conditions:

(A)   An object is good if and only if it is pleasant. (Pleasure and only pleasure is good.)

(B)   An object is better than another if and only if there are differences in the pleasures associated with the two objects that determine their difference in value. (Difference in value is determined by differences in pleasure.)

(C)   An object is better than another if and only if (all things considered) it is more pleasant. (Always, the more pleasure the better.)

This last condition can in turn be split up into two conditions.

(C1)   Differences of pleasure that determine differences of value are always differences that are relevant to whether an object is more or less pleasant.

(C2)   With respect to differences of pleasure that determine differences of value that are also differences relevant to whether an object is more or less pleasant, always the more pleasant the better.

Any theory which meets these two (or three) conditions I shall provisionally call a hedonistic theory of value. Bentham's "quantitative" hedonism satisfies all three of these conditions because it also satisfies a fourth,

(D)   An object is better than another if and only if it is associated with a greater quantity of pleasure. (Always, the greater quantity of pleasure the better.)

The generalized form of the problem I am interested in can now be stated as follows. Must (D) be added to (A)–(C) as a necessary condition of hedonism? In particular, does (D) follow from (A)–(C) or from (A)–(C) together with some other well-founded premiss(es)? As I shall try to make clear, I think the major criticisms that have been directed against Mill amount to the claim that Mill's rejection of (D) is incompatible with something like (A)–(C). I shall defend Mill by arguing that (D) does not follow from (A)–(C), or that if it does, then (C) need not be taken as a necessary condition of hedonism. In particular, (C1) can be given up.

III

What are the arguments that critics have used to try to show that Mill is inconsistent? In this section I shall consider two arguments that rest on Mill's own particular way of stating his qualitative hedonism. In succeeding sections I shall consider arguments that can be generalized to cover any proposed form of qualitative hedonism. It is these latter arguments which I take to be the most interesting criticisms of Mill.

The first argument is due to Mill's own description of what a difference in quality of pleasure amounts to. He says,

> If I am asked what I mean by a difference of quality in pleasures, or what makes one pleasure more valuable than another, merely as a pleasure, except its being greater in amount, there is but one possible answer. Of two pleasures, if there be one to which all or almost all who have experience of both give a decided preference, irrespective of any feeling of moral obligation to prefer it, that is the more desirable pleasure.[11]

Now not only does this *not* provide an account of what a difference in quality of pleasure amounts to, it actually seems to substitute something other than pleasure as the determining factor of value, viz., what an experienced judge would prefer.[12] The passage seems to be an almost explicit abandonment of hedonism.

Despite its appearances, however, this remark of Mill's can, and I think should, be interpreted as providing a way of picking out qualitatively higher pleasures, a way which, although it does not specify the qualitative difference between pleasures that makes them qualitatively higher or lower, nevertheless presupposes the existence of such a difference. That this is so can be seen if we draw an analogy between determining the relative value of pleasures and determining the relative value of wines. If someone who knows very little about wine wants to know how to pick out good wines, he may be told to rely on the preference of certain wine-tasting experts. If those on whom he relies are experts, he will have a way of picking out good wines. But these experts will provide such a guide only if there are some differences between good and bad wines, differences of say, body, bouquet, dryness, etc., which because of their developed senses the experts are able to discriminate. That is, what makes these people experts is their ability to distinguish just those differences which mark off good wines from bad wines. Their expertise presupposes something other than their preference as a basis for the relative merit of wines. Similarly Mill can be interpreted in the passage just quoted as providing a guide for determining higher or lower quality pleasures by reference to certain "pleasure-experts," a guide that even though it does not specify the differences between pleasures that determine whether they are higher or lower quality pleasures, nevertheless presupposes the existence of such a difference. As long as this difference is a difference of pleasure, Mill's theory has yet to be shown to be inconsistent.

But what is this difference of pleasure that provides a basis for determining the relative value of higher and lower quality pleasures?

---

[11] *Utilitarianism, op. cit.*, p. 12.
[12] Both Moore, *op. cit.*, and Bradley, *op. cit.*, seem to subscribe to this argument.

If there is none, then is Mill not forced to look to something quite apart from the pleasure associated with two objects to determine their relative value? Mill does provide a clue for specifying the difference between higher and lower quality pleasures, and that is that higher quality pleasures are "intellectual" or "mental" whereas lower quality pleasures are "sensual."[13] If we assume that there is a difference in the "feel" of intellectual and sensual pleasures,[14] then there will be a qualitative difference between pleasures that can provide a basis for determining the relative value of higher and lower quality pleasures; Mill will not have to look to something other than pleasure to determine the relative value of objects.

A second argument against the consistency of Mill's hedonism turns on his use of the terms "higher" and "lower." To talk about a higher quality pleasure as opposed to a lower quality pleasure is not yet to pick out any aspect of pleasure similar to that, say, of intensity, that admits of higher or lower amounts, higher or lower degrees. Unless there is some aspect of pleasure such intensity which admits of higher amounts of degrees, the terms "higher" and "lower" have no meaning. And if they have no meaning, then Mill can point to no difference of pleasure that accounts for the difference of value between higher and lower quality pleasures. If he can point to no such difference, then he must rely on something other than pleasure as a basis for judgments of comparative value.[15]

However, even if one grants that "higher" and "lower" do not all by themselves serve as a basis for picking out any differences in the quality of pleasure that can serve as a basis for judgments of comparative value, this is not enough to convict Mill of inconsistency. The most damaging conclusion one can draw from this admission is that Mill has not *specified* the difference between higher and lower quality pleasures. It does not follow from this that there is no such difference. Furthermore, as I have already suggested, Mill does provide a hint at what he takes to be the difference between higher and lower quality pleasures, and that is the difference between "intellectual" and "sensual" pleasures. Mill's use of the terms "higher" and "lower" to refer to qualitative differences between pleasures is not, therefore, enough to convict him of inconsistency.

[13] See e.g., *Utilitarianism, op. cit.*, pp. 11–12.
[14] This, of course, is an assumption that can and should be called into question, but there are grounds for thinking that Mill did make this assumption. Even if the assumption turns out to be false, it will not be enough to convict Mill of inconsistency; he simply would have held a false view about pleasure.
[15] Bradley, *op. cit.*, seems to be offering an argument similar to this against Mill.

IV

The replies I have given to the two arguments in the previous section seem to assume that all that Mill needs to be consistent is to be able to point to some qualitative difference between pleasures which, according to him provides a basis for judgments of comparative value. What this amounts to is the assumption that conditions (A) and (B) are all that are necessary for hedonism. But is this assumption correct? There is another condition besides (A) and (B) which I have suggested as a necessary condition of hedonism, condition (C); qualitative hedonism may be incompatible with (C).

This brings me to the first of the arguments against Mill that can be generalized to fit any form of qualitative hedonism—that Mill is committed by his qualitative hedonism to denying that an object associated with a greater amount of pleasure is always better than an object associated with a lesser amount of pleasure, and *this denial* is inconsistent with hedonism. Ewing puts the objection this way,

> To say that pleasure is the only good and yet admit that a lesser pleasure may be preferable to a greater is like saying that money is the only thing which counts and then adding that money earned by public work is better than the same amount of money earned by business. If pleasure is the only good, the more pleasure always the better.[16]

John Hospers reports the same sort of objection when he says,

> According to some critics, however, this "qualitative" principle of Mill's is a blunder: partly because if something is (in the long run) *less* pleasurable and yet better, then one has already deserted pleasure as the sole criterion of desirability. . . . [17]

Stated in terms of the results of Section II this objection is that the denial of (D) is incompatible with (C). But what reason is there to think that the denial of (D) is incompatible with (C)? The argument which I think lies behind objections like those of Ewing and Hospers is something like the following.

Suppose (C) is a necessary condition of hedonism. Then for any two objects x and y,

(1) x is better than y if and only if (all things considered) x is more pleasant than y.

Suppose now (D) is false, and that the greater pleasure is not always the better. Then it will be possible for there to be two objects x and y such that

(2) x is better than y,

[16] *Ethics, op. cit.*, pp. 42–43.
[17] *Human Conduct, op. cit.*, p. 59.

but

(3) It is not the case that x has a greater quantity of pleasure than y.

From (1) and (2) it follows that

(4) (All things considered) x is more pleasant than y.

However, for any two objects x and y,

(5) x has a greater quantity of pleasure than y if and only if x is more pleasant than y.

From (3) and (5) it follows that

(6) It is not the case that x is more pleasant than y,

and (6) contradicts (4). On the assumption that (C) is a necessary condition of hedonism, Mill's denial of (D) results in a contradiction; therefore, his qualitative hedonism is inconsistent.

Despite its appearances I do not think that the above argument shows that Mill is inconsistent. In fact, I think it comes quite close to begging the question against Mill. The culprit here is premiss (5). Although I think there is a way of understanding

(5a) If x has a greater quantity of pleasure than y, then x is more pleasant than y,

so that it is true, it is by no means clear that

(5b) If x is more pleasant than y, then x has a greater quantity of pleasure than y,

is true, or that it is a premiss that Mill would concede to his critics. It is (5b) that carries the inference from (3) to (6). (5b) would be true if the only way one object could be more pleasant than another would be for it to have a greater quantity of pleasure than the other, but to maintain this in the present context comes close to begging the question against Mill. Suppose, for the sake of argument, that there are differences in the quality of pleasures that provide a basis for saying that one object is better than another, i.e., suppose that Mill's qualitative hedonism is correct. This assumption is warranted in the present context, since if the above argument works at all, it works as a *reductio* of Mill's position. I see no reason why, on this assumption, one would not talk about one object being *qualitatively more pleasant* than another. Despite the initially odd sound of "qualitatively more pleasant," not every use of the comparative "more" is one that rests on a difference of quantity. Not every use of "more" is replaceable by "a greater amount of," or "a greater quantity of." For example, if I say that Smith is more graceful than Jones, I am not saying that he has a greater quantity of gracefulness than Jones or that he has a greater quantity of anything else than Jones. Let us call such a use of "more" a *qualitative* use of "more"; and let us call a use of "more" which can be replaced by "a greater quantity of" a *quantitative* use of "more." Then, *if* there are qualitative differences of pleasure that have a bearing on the comparative value of objects, I see no reason for thinking that an object cannot be qualitatively more pleasant than another as well as being quantitatively more pleasant. If this is so, then (5b) and therefore (5) turn out to be false, and the contradiction derived in the above argument simply does not follow from the denial of (D). The only way to maintain (5) would be to hold either that an object which is quantitatively more pleasant is always all things considered more pleasant, and given Mill's rejection of (D) this certainly is something he would not concede to his critics, or to hold that there is no such thing as an object's being qualitatively more pleasant than another. In the absence of further argument this latter claim could only rest on the denial that qualitative differences of pleasures bear on the relative value of objects, and it is precisely this which is at issue.

One may be unhappy over my introduction of the notion of a qualitative "more" or the notion of something's being qualitatively more pleasant, and to some extent I share a certain uneasiness about this sort of talk. However, given that the above argument is supposed to be a *reductio* of Mill's position, independent grounds have to be given for not allowing this sort of talk, for it certainly is something that is suggested by Mill's theory. Until such independent grounds are given, any attempt to rule it out will smack of question-begging. However, even if one does not buy this defense of Mill, there is another that can be mustered on his behalf which makes the above unnecessary, and that is that (C) need not be taken as a necessary condition of hedonism. That it is possible for (C) to be consistently denied by a hedonist is something that will emerge in Section VI.

V

Despite the inadequacy of the argument in Section IV one may still feel that Mill's claim that qualitative differences of pleasure have a bearing on the relative value of objects surruptitiously introduces a new standard or criterion of value other than pleasure. As Abelson puts it,

> . . . Mill's criterion of quality introduces a standard of value other than pleasure, by which pleasure itself can be evaluated, and thus contradicts the principle of utility, that pleasure is the single standard of good.[18]

The argument which I think lies behind this objection is something like the following.

[18] See n. 7.

Suppose that qualitative hedonism is true, and that for some objects x and y, x is better than y because x is associated with a higher quality of pleasure than y. Then it follows from (B) that

(7) There is some difference in quality between the pleasures associated with x and y that accounts for their difference in value. There is some quality of pleasure ϕ, such that the pleasure associated with x has ϕ and the pleasure associated with y does not, or the pleasure associated with x has a greater degree of ϕ than the pleasure associated with y.

Since by hypothesis both x and y are pleasant, x and y cannot differ simply in the fact that x is pleasant and y is not. Therefore,

(8) ϕ is something other than pleasure.

It also follows from (7) that the difference between the pleasures associated with x and y determines the difference in value between x and y. But this can be true only if

(9) Being ϕ or having a certain degree of ϕ is, everything else being equal, valuable.

For how could there be more value associated with x than y unless there was something associated with x but not y that was valuable? However, it follows from (8) and (9) that

(10) Something other than pleasure, namely ϕ or a certain degree of ϕ, is valuable.

This contradicts (A), the condition that pleasure and only pleasure is valuable.

There are two considerations which show, I think, that the above argument is not correct. The first is that one can construct a parallel argument with the same logical form in which one can admit the analogues of (7) and (8) and yet deny the analogue of (10). The second is that if the above argument shows that qualitative hedonism is inconsistent, it also shows that quantitative hedonism is inconsistent, and the latter view does not seem to be inconsistent.

As analogue to questions about comparative value I suggest we take questions about comparative visibility, and as analogue to hedonism I suggest we take the following theory of visibility, what I shall call the color theory of visibility. An object is visible if and only if it is colored. Differences in visibility are determined entirely by differences in color, in particular by the differences in the amount of color possessed by a given object (something which would normally be measured by the surface area of the colored portion of the object) and differences in the brightness of color possessed by a given object. Everything else being equal, the greater the amount of color associated with a given object the more visible the object, and, everything else being equal, the brighter the color associated with a given object the more visible the object. According to the color theory of visibility, the comparative visibility of two objects is determined by both qualitative and quantitative differences in color. *Prima facie* the color theory of visibility is consistent.

Consider now the following argument. Suppose that the color theory of visibility holds and that there are two objects x and y such that x is more visible than y because of some difference in the quality of the colors of x and y. Then it will be true that

(7′) There is some difference in the quality of the colors of x and y that accounts for their difference in visibility, in particular a difference in brightness. The color associated with x is brighter than that associated with y,

and

(8′) Brightness is something different from color. (Being bright is not the same as being colored.)

However, does it follow that

(9′) To have a certain degree of brightness is, everything else being equal, to be visible,

and, therefore, that

(10′) Something other than color, brightness, is visible?

I think not. If anything follows from (7′) and (8′) it is that *bright color* is visible, not that brightness *per se* is visible. To see that this is so, suppose that objects which are not colored also have various degrees of brightness. Suppose that sounds as well as colors are bright. We do somethimes say that a violinist has an especially bright tone or that certain stops on an organ give it a bright sound.[19] If (7′) and (8′)

---

[19] One might object that sounds are not bright in the same *sense* that colors are, but even if this is so, it is irrelevant for my purpose. The point I want to make can still be made if one assumes for the sake of argument that sounds are bright in the same sense as colors are bright. What is at issue is whether the introduction of qualitative differences in pleasure as a basis for differences in value brings with it a standard of value other than pleasure, and my argument that it does not will go through if one grants that things other than pleasure can admit of the qualitative differences which when they are differences of pleasure determine differences in value, but these things are not thereby made valuable. In the second place even if the qualitative differences in pleasure that make a difference to value are *necessarily* differences of pleasure, the best a critic could do would be to achieve a stand-off, for if this were so there would be no reason for thinking that the differences all by themselves were valuable or whether they are valuable only as differences of pleasure. Finally I think it may be possible to argue that if the qualitative differences of pleasure that determine differences in value are necessarily differences of pleasure, then the view that these differences are valuable by themselves is equivalent to the view that pleasure is valuable. If this is so, then the view that these differences are valuable in themselves would not be inconsistent with hedonism; it would be a restatement of hedonism.

actually did lead to (9') and (10'), then someone who held the color theory of visibility would be committed to the view that sounds having a certain degree of brightness are visible. But this is absurd, and someone holding the color theory of visibility can consistently deny it. It is not the brightness that a color has which all by itself makes an object that has that color visible; it is the *brightness-of-color*. That is, what follows from (7') and (8') is not (9') but

(9'') To have a certain degree of bright color is, everything else being equal, to be visible,

and (10') does not follow from (8') and (9''). All the color theory of visibility commits one to is that *bright colors* are visible; it does not commit one to the view that something other than color, namely brightness, is visible.

Similarly I think a hedonist can admit that even though a pleasure with a certain degree of some quality ϕ is valuable and that the quality ϕ is not the same as the quality of being pleasant, it does not follow that something other than pleasure, namely ϕ, is valuable. All the qualitative hedonist is committed to is that *pleasures* with a certain degree of ϕ are valuable, and this is consistent with hedonism, at least as long as he also maintains that objects which are not pleasant that also have a certain degree of ϕ are not valuable.

A second reason for thinking that the argument from (7) and (8) to (10) is not valid, is that if it were, it would also show that Bentham's quantitative hedonism is inconsistent. If two pleasures differ in quantity, then there must be some difference between them other than that one is pleasant and the other is not, e.g., a difference of intensity, a difference which would account for a difference in value between the two pleasures. However, this does not show that Bentham or anyone else holding a similar view is committed to the view that something other than pleasure, namely a certain degree of intensity, is valuable. All that follows is that more intense pleasures are better than less intense pleasures. If the argument would not be taken as showing that quantitative hedonism is inconsistent, then why should it be taken as showing that qualitative hedonism is inconsistent?

One might suspect that since the above argument is one which, if it were correct, would work against quantitative as well as qualitative hedonism, it is not really the argument which is behind criticisms that Mill is inconsistent. Either the above argument can be supplemented to show that Mill is inconsistent or there is another argument that shows that Mill is inconsistent.

Garner and Rosen suggest a supplemented version when they say,

If two things vary in their desirability, there must be some factor (not itself without value) that makes the difference. If so, and if pleasure alone is valuable, only an addition of pleasure could bring about an increase in the value of anything. Bentham accepts this but Mill does not, and therefore Mill is sometimes criticized as being inconsistent.[20]

What these remarks suggest is something like the following. Any difference in the value of two objects must rest on some difference between them. Either this difference can be specified solely in terms of pleasure, or the difference must be specified in terms of something other than pleasure. Only the first of these alternatives is consistent with hedonism. Quantitative hedonism falls within this first alternative, because a difference of quantity of pleasure is simply an addition of pleasure. However, in order to specify some difference in the *quality* of two pleasures, one must resort to something other than pleasure to specify this difference, and this immediately introduces something else as a basis of value.

If this is a fair way of paraphrasing Garner and Rosen's remarks, then I think that this argument does not show that qualitative hedonism is inconsistent. The question that needs to be answered is how one is to specify a difference between two objects using only the notion of pleasure, when by hypothesis both objects are pleasant. The answer, I think, is that one cannot do it. Even if the difference is only that of quantity of pleasure, before one can talk about a difference of quantity of pleasure he must be able to specify the dimensions or aspects of pleasure that admit of quantitative measurement. Unless there was some dimension of pleasure like intensity that admits of quantitative measurement, it would be impossible to talk about different quantities of pleasure. Thus, the specification of a difference of quantity of pleasure requires reference to concepts other than pleasure, concepts like intensity. If this is enough to make a view inconsistent with hedonism, then quantitative hedonism is inconsistent. But quantitative hedonism is not inconsistent. Therefore, the fact that one must make reference to something other than pleasure when specifying the difference in quality of pleasures that determines a difference in their value, does not make qualitative hedonism inconsistent.

One may still feel that I am being obtuse, that I am simply refusing to see that there is something about qualitative hedonism that sets it apart from quantitative hedonism and makes it inconsistent. But if so, what is it? One suggestion might be that quantitative hedonism satisfies condition (C), but qualitative hedonism does not. Differences

[20] *Moral Philosophy, op. cit.*, p. 153.

of quantity of pleasure are those which determine whether an object is *more* pleasant than another; differences in quality are not. Insofar as quantitative differences can be specified as differences of more or less pleasure, then for quantitative hedonism there is a sense in which one can specify those factors which determine the difference in value between two objects by using only the concept of pleasure—they are differences of more or less pleasure. This is not so for qualitative hedonism. However, this suggestion does no more than reintroduce an argument that has already been considered and rejected in Section IV. Given that there is a qualitative use of "more" there is no reason why differences in the quality of two pleasures cannot also be differences that determine whether one object is more pleasant than another.

IV

This last suggestion, however, raises the final argument that I want to consider in this paper. It may be granted that "more" has a quantitative use as well as a qualitative use in that there are some characteristics for which if one object has more of that characteristic than another, then it has a greater amount of that characteristic than the other, whereas there are other characteristics for which this is not so. Nevertheless it may be maintained that there is no characteristic which admits of more or less for which it is appropriate to use *both* the qualitative and the quantitative uses of "more." That is, one may maintain that the following is true,

(E) For any characteristic ϕ, if there is a use of "more" in which "x is more ϕ than y" implies "x has a greater amount of ϕ than y," then *every* use of "x is more ϕ than y" has this implication.

Given (E) and given that pleasure admits of a quantitative use of "more," then it follows that there is no difference in the quality of pleasures that will make one object more pleasant than another. From this and condition (C) it follows that qualitative hedonism is inconsistent.

In order to see that this last objection need not be taken seriously, all one has to do is to recall the color theory of visibility. According to this theory there are both quantitative and qualitative differences between colors that determine the relative visibility of an object—the amount of color and its brightness. What is of interest here is that there is at least one use of "more" according to which what has more color is, everything else being equal, more visible, and that is when an object has a greater amount of color than another. That is, color admits of a quantitative use of "more." But what are we to say when an object has a brighter color than another? Is it also "more colored?" My linguistic intuitions are not entirely clear here, but what is important to realize is that no matter what answer one gives to this question, the analogue of one of the premisses of the last objection, (E) or (C), will have to be given up. If one is prepared to say that a brighter color does have more color than one that is not so bright, then there are some properties that admit of both the qualitative and quantitative use of "more," and (E) is false. Furthermore, if this can be true of color, then why not also for pleasure? On the other hand, if one says that an object with a brighter color does not have more color (and this is what I am inclined to say), then the analogue of (C)

(C′) An object is more visible than another if and only if it has more color,

is false. And if (C′) is not necessary for a theory of comparative visibility according to which color and only color is visible, then why should (C) be necessary for a theory of comparative value according to which pleasure and only pleasure is valuable? Either way the above objection does not show that qualitative hedonism is inconsistent.

It is important to note that if one ends up rejecting (C) because of considerations like those above (and I think this is the most reasonable line to take), he does not have to give up (C2). He is only committed to giving up (C1), the view that the differences of pleasure that determine differences of value are always differences that are relevant to whether an object is more or less pleasant. This is important, since (C2) rules out as a form of hedonism the view that the lesser the pleasure the better. An argument that qualitative hedonism is consistent based on a conception of hedonism according to which the view that the lesser the pleasure the better is a form of hedonism would be far less interesting than one according to which qualitative hedonism is consistent and this latter theory of comparative value is ruled out as a form of hedonism.

I conclude that there is no reason to think that Mill's qualitative hedonism is inconsistent, and that as long as a theory fulfills conditions (A), (B), and (C2), there are good reasons for calling it a form of hedonism. There is, of course, always the chance that there is an argument that I have not considered that would show that qualitative hedonism is inconsistent, but arguments cannot be considered until they are raised. As with charges of legal wrong-doing, I think a person should be presumed innocent of inconsistency until proven otherwise.

University of Minnesota

Recent Work on Ethical Naturalism

R. L. FRANKLIN

I. MEANINGS AND STARTING POINTS

I use the word "naturalism" because moral philosophers refuse to pension it off. It has at least two major senses, each of which is imprecise, and each of which on any interpretation is a name for many problems. This survey is concerned with only one sense, and with only some of the problems raised thereby

Naturalism$_1$ refers to normative claims that moral issues can be settled by empirically or scientifically ascertainable facts, rather than by appeal to the will of God, intuited moral absolutes, etc. Naturalism$_2$ is a thesis in meta-ethics that ethical judgments are statements of fact. These are cross-classifications. E.g., an anti-naturalist$_2$ is opposed to *any* theory which treats moral judgments as statements of fact, even of non-naturalist$_1$ fact. Yet he may hold that moral judgments, though not statements of fact, are rendered more or less appropriate by facts, and may also hold that the facts in question could be empirically ascertained. Then in tone and practical import he may be indistinguishable from naturalists$_1$.[1] In the past decade naturalism$_1$ has received little attention.[2] Naturalism$_2$ has been a storm centre, involving what are called the "is/ought question" and the "fact/value

[1] Some anti-naturalists$_2$ tie "true" and "false" to statements of fact, and so conclude that moral judgments are neither true nor false; though (some will add) there may be good reasons for accepting or rejecting them. Others, agreeing with the latter point, tie "true" and "false" to good reasons for acceptance or rejection, and thus call moral judgments true or false. Some stricter anti-naturalists$_2$ hold that even to grant that facts are relevant to moral judgments in the above sense makes one a naturalist$_2$ in disguise. On the other hand, E. M. Adams (190), in the process of arguing for a form of non-naturalism$_1$ treats "naturalism," as covering all views which require only scientifically investigatable entities in their ontology. This makes all the anti-naturalist views I shall discuss—those of R. M. Hare, etc.—forms of naturalism. (Numbers in parentheses refer to those listings in the Bibliography.)

[2] The centenary of Dewey's birth in 1960 produced some discussions of his ethics; cf. R. W. Sleeper (155), E. A. Burtt (17), A. E. Murphy (120), G. Kennedy (85), J. A. Irving (78), S. M. Eames (32). W. K. Frankena (42) and C. A. Baylis (10) have discussed C. I. Lewis. On issues connected with naturalism$_1$ generally, cf. R. W. Sellars (149), Y. H. Krikorian (88), P. J. Olscamp (128), M. R. Cohen (202), D. H. Monro (227), R. B. Perry (232), J. P. Johnson (80), E. F. Walter (181), B. Blanshard (199), D. W. Gotshalk (213), S. C. Pepper (231) and (230), and P. B. Rice (239).

question." This is my area of concern, which in general I call "naturalism" without a subscript.

English-speaking debates about naturalism are still entangled in a history which goes back to G. E. Moore's *Principia Ethica* (228) in 1903, and to his polemic against the Naturalistic Fallacy.[3] Moore argued against the utilitarians that goodness was a simple, "non-natural" (i.e., non-empirical) quality, and thus could not be identified with the "natural" quality of happiness. This seems to be anti-naturalism. But he also held that to identify goodness with any *non*-natural quality than itself was to commit exactly the same fallacy; which may seem to be anti-naturalism$_2$. His arguments mostly required a theory of language which few successors found defensible, but philosophers of later generations took him to have enunciated two fundamental anti-naturalist points: (1) that we cannot legitimately move from empirical or factual judgments to normative or value ones (cf. his distinction between natural and non-natural qualities); (2) that any attempt to show something was good or right by *defining* "good" or "right" in such a way that the desired conclusion would follow, could prove nothing (cf. his insistence that "good" is indefinable).

At a later date, Moore's insistence that "good" did not name a natural quality tended to be seen through positivist eyes as a confused recognition that ethical judgments were not empirical, hence not verifiable, hence not statements of fact at all.[4] This was reinforced by the logically independent argument that moral language must be action-guiding; i.e., that it must answer the question "What shall I do?", and that no statement of fact could do that. Indeed the Naturalistic Fallacy was often taken to be that of assuming that factual statements could be action guiding.[5] The fundamental issue now became not Moore's problem: "Granted that ethical propositions are *sui*

---

[3] For the continental history, cf. J. P. Johnson (81) and N. Rescher (236) (Ch. V). For general indications of Moore's influence, cf. A. W. Levi (93), G. Franks (46) and (47), P. Foot (210), G. Warnock (252), M. Warnock (253), H. H. Cox (26). On Moore's own version of the Naturalistic Fallacy, see especially C. L. Stevenson (168), G. E. Moore (118), W. K. Frankena (43), G. Nakhnikian (121), R. W. Sellars (149), B. Kuklick (89), B. H. Baumrin (9), C. D. Broad (15), D. P. Gauthier (49), D. Mitchell (110), A. N. Prior (234), R. Brandt (200), G. O. Allen (2), E. H. Duncan (30), G. Bergmann (12), R. Hancock (59), R. G. Durrant (31), E. M. Adams (190), P. W. Taylor (248), B. Mayo (225). For the discussion of the Fallacy in general, see n. 41 at beginning of Sect. 4. Discussions of R. M. Hare's version of the Fallacy are cited later in Sect. 4.

[4] This stage also marks the rejection of normative ethics, whereas Moore's ultimate aim had been to find out what things in fact were good.

[5] If this seems a far cry from the fallacy of claiming to define an indefinable quality, it may be that by this time more philosophers were prepared to pay tribute to Moore than to read him carefully.

generis, what sorts of things are in fact good?"; but rather: "Granted that ethical utterances do not state propositions, what do they do?". The two principal answers to the new question were that they were expressions of emotion, and that they were disguised commands: i.e., the emotivist and prescriptivist (or imperativist) theories of ethics. The debates in the 1960's turn primarily on prescriptivism.[6]

In the last decade another historical influence has become important: the final paragraph of Bk. III Pt. I, Sect. I of Hume's *Treatise*, where he remarks that it "seems altogether inconceivable" that "from the usual copulations of propositions, *is*, and *is not*" there could be a deduction of a proposition "connected with an *ought* or an *ought not*." Many have concluded that to say that an "ought" cannot be deduced from an "is" is essentially the same as to say that we cannot derive value judgments from factual premisses, and is yet another version of the Naturalistic Fallacy.

Finally, another intertwining debate in moral philosophy throughout the 1960's is about what I shall call objectivism and subjectivism.[7] An objectivist in this sense asserts, and a subjectivist denies, that there are at least sometimes ultimately better reasons for one moral view than for alternatives. Early emotive and prescriptive views were subjectivist. Yet to most philosophers in the 1960's a thorough-going subjectivism seemed to make ethics implausibly irrational, and to leave no room for any distinction between moral discussion and propaganda. This reaction took two radically different meta-ethical forms, round which this survey revolves: (1) the development of more sophisticated anti-naturalist theories aiming to show that though moral judgments did not state facts they might yet be rationally defensible; (2) the questioning of anti-naturalism itself.

I examine (1) by discussing in Sect. 2 the best known claim to objective non-naturalism, that of R. M. Hare. I must largely pass over important subsidiary issues raised by other anti-naturalists: e.g., by those who insist on a distinction between prescription and evaluation, though Hare reduces the latter to the former; and by those who insist that the multiplicity of tasks which moral utterances perform cannot be reduced to any simple model.[8]

---

[6] I shall not discuss the emotive theory. Apart from its *locus classicus*, C. L. Stevenson's *Ethics and Language* (246), cf. H. N. Castaneda esp. (20), J. T. Wilcox (185), J. N. Garver (48), C. Wellman (182), C. L. Stevenson (247) and especially J. O. Urmson (250).

[7] For uses of "subjectivism" different to mine see, e.g., A. J. Ayer (195), P. Edwards (209), R. Brandt (200).

[8] Cf. B. Mayo (225), J. Hartland-Swan (218), P. W. Taylor (248) and (174), P. H. Nowell-Smith (229).

E

As to (2), the basic aim of the naturalist counter-attack is to remove the alleged radical gulf between value and fact. A common strategy is to argue that a given term both is undeniably evaluative and also has what I shall call a fixed descriptive content. The latter phrase means that the descriptive content, i.e., what the term applies to in the world, is not fixed merely by the speaker's attitudes etc. If the strategy succeeds, then for that term it will be true as a matter of sheer linguistic fact, both that it is applicable to a situation because of its descriptive content, and also that it conveys an evaluation.

This strategy has been applied in various areas, and here too I have had to be selective. Thus some naturalists have paid particular attention to *specific* moral notions such as rudeness, pride, and courage, which may seem to have more obviously both an evaluative force and a fixed descriptive content.[9] There is also debate about the meaning of "moral" itself; where naturalists assert that to speak of a moral principle not related to human wants or needs would be to abuse language, while anti-naturalists reject this fixed descriptive content by definining the word in terms of whatever a man accepts as ultimately binding.[10] I discuss the strategy, however, only in connection with "ought" and "good" (Sects. 3 and 4). For I think that in every case certain standard anti-naturalist defenses arise. A man who does not wish to condemn rudeness, or who has a set of overriding principles paying no primary attention to human wants, may: (1) refuse to use the word in question; (2) use it in a purely "inverted commas" sense, indicating that it is what his society would call rude, moral, etc., but that he does not agree with the judgment; or (3) alter the denotation of the term by redefinition, saying "real courage is . . . ."[11] And these issues also arise in relation to "ought" or "good."[12]

[9] This approach is found particularly in the articles of P. Foot and also of G. E. M. Anscombe. It may perhaps be inspired partly by Aristotle's discussion of separate virtues, and also by J. L. Austin's interest in less commonly discussed notions (cf. (194), pp. 126–127). For a sophisticated discussion of "malice" which is close to Searle's position on "ought" (Sect. 3), see J. D. Wallace (180).

[10] For a naturalist position cf. G. Warnock (252). On the question of the nature of morality generally, cf. *inter alia* Castaneda & Nakhnikian (201), and especially Frankena (*ibid.*) and his bibliography. For an attempt of mine to analyze the notion in terms of six jointly sufficient criteria, any one of which might be absent on any one occasion, see (211), p. 209.

[11] On these points cf. Hare ((62); see (220), p. 246), (216), pp. 164,187–189, (217), pp. 124–126, 145–149; A. G. N. Flew ((38); see (220), p. 139); R. V. Hannaford (61). For a real willingness to abandon the word "moral" if necessary to make his point, cf. J. J. C. Smart, ((161); see (210), p. 182).

[12] I have also had to ignore many other relevant issues, E.g.: (1) The same naturalist principle is one element in the debate about whether there are logical limits to what a man can want. Cf. Anscombe (192), Hare ((62); see (220), pp. 247–252). (2) Because it has been relatively little discussed I ignore, though I impliedly

Within my chosen field, the most notable feature of the debate has been its indecisiveness. The protagonists come in general from the same tradition, they argue in the same sort of way, and in terms of sheer debating skill they are most equally matched. Yet they remain sturdily unconvinced. I think the explanation is twofold. Firstly there is the usual failure to distinguish the distinguishable, so that a position is defended *in toto* because its central claim seems vital. Secondly the debate cannot, I believe, be solved as a matter of ethics at all. For in several dimensions it leads on to other issues, and so the answer given will depend on answers given or assumed to other, not specifically ethical, problems.

2. R. M. HARE'S PRESCRIPTIVISM

Hare's two books, *The Language of Morals* (217) in 1952 and *Freedom and Reason* (216) in 1963, are so much at the heart of the debate that I refer to them henceforth as LM and FR respectively. There and elsewhere he presents a position combining an extreme simplicity in its two basic principles with a sophisticated ingenuity in their elaboration.

The first principle is the basic anti-naturalist distinction between statements of fact and action-guiding language. Hare identifies the latter with imperatives or commands.

a statement, however loosely it is bound to the facts, cannot answer a question of the form "What shall I do?"; only a command can do this.[13]

His final terminology is (FR, pp. 26–27) that if an expression has nothing but descriptive meaning it is descriptive; if it has *any* prescriptive meaning it is prescriptive; if it has both kinds it is evaluative. Thus evaluatives are a sub-class of prescriptives.

The second principle is universalizability, which aims to confer objectivity on ethics. If a descriptive word applies to a situation it must apply to any other relevantly similar one. This is true of an evaluative term because it, too, has descriptive meaning. But since it also has prescriptive meaning, and entails imperatives about how to

---

disagree with G. H. von Wright's claim that there is no specifically moral good among *The Varieties of Goodness* (251). (3) I must also ignore debates about the relevance of scientific discovery for ethics. On this point I am inclined to think the most under-discussed books are those of A. Edel (see, e.g. (204–7)).

[13] LM, p. 46; cf. p. 79, Hare recognizes that there are other sorts of meaning besides prescriptive and descriptive (e.g., LM, chap. 1; FR, chap. 2 esp. pp. 9–10). But he is convinced that an adequate account of moral language can be given in terms of this pair of concepts.

act, to agree that it correctly applies to a situation commits one to agreeing, not merely that any other such situation must be similarly described, but further that in any such situation a man, including oneself, ought to act in the appropriate way. To agree that X is the morally appropriate thing to do entails assenting to the first-person singular imperative addressed to oneself, "Let me do X."[14]

Thus, for Hare, we have on the one hand a complete moral freedom. Our community's moral vocabulary will have an established descriptive meaning, yet, contrary to naturalist views, we do not use these terms in a fully moral sense until we adopt them for ourselves, by assenting to the imperative, "Let me act like this" (cf., e.g., LM, p. 70). This fundamental principle I shall call the thesis of moral autonomy (see esp. Sect. 5). It is intimately linked with his version of the Naturalistic Fallacy (LM, pp. 81 et seq.; see Sect. 4): that if "good" had a purely "natural," i.e., descriptive meaning, it could not be used to commend. Yet, on the other hand, universalizability requires a man to accept only imperatives which he would be prepared to have applied by others to himself as well as by himself to others. This places Hare within a diverse family of theories (e.g., K. Baier (197), M. G. Singer (244)), which have Kant as their common ancestor.

Hare has been attacked from many directions. There is criticism of his doctrine of the logic of imperatives, and of his tendency to use "imperative" and "command" virtually interchangeably. [15] This issue certainly needs clarification, but I here assume what I take to be Hare's basic position: that the perspicuous, unpuzzling case of action-guiding language is the grammatical imperative; and that therefore any illuminating account of other action-guiding language must ultimately be reduced to this.[16] To other critics the sheer multiplicity of purposes for which we use moral language (making decisions, evaluating alternatives, advising, praising, etc.), is enough to show

[14] This is the emphasis in FR. In the earlier book (cf. LM, chap. 2) the emphasis was on the claim that logical relations such as contrariety can hold between imperatives.

[15] The whole question of imperative inference has received considerable attention. See the bibliography in N. Rescher (237).

[16] A contrasting terminology is that of B. Mayo (225). He rejects the notion of a command as a model for e.g., an ought-statement ((225), pp. 148–152), and yet holds an imperativist theory of "ought," because he distinguishes sharply between commands and imperatives. But to do so he makes a singular imperative "just anything which gives an answer to the question, 'What shall I do?'" (p. 190) and says that "such sentences need not be in the 'Imperative mood'" (p. 24). I am not sure whether by "imperative" he just means what I later call "a reason for an action," or whether he holds some stronger, but apparently undefended, position that the perspicuous form of such a reason is a grammatical imperative.

that no single model of "prescription" will cover all cases.[17] Others attack his account of the relation of imperatives to action, and particularly the resultant problems over freewill.[18] And there are yet other objections.[19] I concentrate on two issues most basic for the themes I discuss: (a) the distinction between description and prescription, and (b) the notion of a self-addressed command.

(a) *Description/prescription.* Hare says of this distinction that, like the analytic/synthetic one, it is an essential tool of the philosopher.[20] How then does he argue for it? I think that at bottom he never does; that his arguments always presuppose it. Here is a typical passage:

> We can show that such a distinction exists . . . if we can isolate one of these two sorts of meaning in a given context, and show that it does not exhaust the meaning of the term in that context.[21]

He goes on to demonstrate that "X is a good wine" does not mean the same as "X is ϕ," where ϕ are the characteristics which make a good wine. But his argument turns on essentially the point on which Moore relied to prove that "good" names a non-natural quality. Hare's particular account of the difference—viz., that the meaning of "good" retains the content of ϕ and adds a commendation—is simply presupposed.[22]

To many philosophers, however, argument might seem superfluous. Is not the dichotomy established by the fact that we can make and agree upon the distinction in all sorts of contexts? E.g., we can distinguish between ascribing values (stating that A holds them) and subscribing to them (endorsing them ourselves). Certainly we can and must make such distinctions. Yet I suspect they not only fail to establish Hare's position but may be incompatible with it.

[17] E.g., G. Warnock ((252), chap. 4); cf. P. H. Nowell-Smith (229), esp. p. 98); J. Margolis (106). Hare would presumably reply (whether justifiably or not) that he concedes the differences, but has found the criterion which marks off the whole genus of moral language.
[18] For Hare's position see LM, pp. 20, 169 and esp. FR, chap. 5. For criticisms cf. G. Matthews (107), M. C. McGuire (96) and my (211), esp. pp. 229–232. A related issue is whether sincere assent to an imperative entails that I must merely issue an imperative to myself, or that I must actually do the action. Cf. R. Edgley (208).
[20] See Hare ((62) and cf. (220), p. 241). (Indeed he claims [*ibid.*, pp. 240–241, 255] (172), J. A. Brunton (16), A. K. Sen (152), (151), W. E. Morris (119), P. J. Olscamp (127), H. G. Hubbeling (71), E. F. Walter (181), A. C. MacIntyre (98), R. C. Solomon (163), C. D. McNiven (101), R. Hancock (58), F. E. Sparshott (164), J. Kovesi (223), D. Pole ((233), chap. 11). On his version of the Naturalistic Fallacy, cf. Sect. 4, and on universalizability cf. Sect . 5.
[20] See Hare ((62) and cf. (220), p. 241). (Indeed he claims [*ibid.*, pp. 240–241, 255] that it is an offshoot of the analytic/synthetic one.)
[21] *Ibid.*
[22] The passages he cites (*ibid.*, p. 240) as further establishing the doctrine (viz., LM, esp. chap. 7; FR, pp. 22–27, 51, 56), seem to presuppose it in the same way.

They fail to establish it because Hare's account is in terms of the prescriptive and descriptive meaning of *words* (cf., e.g., FR, p. 10) while the useful working distinction is between *sentences* which ascribe or subscribe, etc. Since the same words may appear in each type of sentence, it is not clear how a sentence-meaning distinction can support a word-meaning one. As to the possible incompatibility: the useful distinction not only applies to sentences rather than words, but has its point in *contrasting* them. Hare's position is that evaluative terms have *both* descriptive *and* prescriptive meaning in every normal use, but if every typical ascriptive sentence also had subscriptive meaning, then the useful distinction would disappear.

If the required descriptive/prescriptive distinction is neither argued for nor undeniable, where does it come from? I suspect it is an offshoot, not of the analytic/synthetic distinction but of the use the Positivists made of it.[23] Positivists were interested almost exclusively in statements, and scarcely cared whether moral utterances were called prescriptive, evaluative, or emotive. Anti-naturalist moral philosophers may easily have been influenced in two ways. Firstly, as P. Foot contends, when concentrating their interest on moral utterances they may have assumed too easily that the notion of a description was clear.[24] Secondly they may easily have assumed that there was a basic *single* element in non-statements, corresponding to empirical verifiability in the cognitively meaningful. Both these suggestions lead to the issues raised in Sect. 6. Brief remarks like the above can carry little weight until a better account of action-guiding language is proposed, but I conclude that the fundamental prescriptive/descriptive distinction needs more argument than prescriptivism assumes.

(b) *Self-addressed commands.* I have already noted how fundamental is Hare's principle of autonomy: that we must accept for ourselves our moral principles. One consequence surely is that an ordinary command or imperative cannot, in the required sense, answer the question "What shall I do?" As a statement of fact, for any non-naturalist, always leaves open the question "But what is that to me?", so a command leaves open the question "But shall I obey it?" What is needed, at least for a moral decision, is a *self-addressed* command, "Let me do X."

Hence the imperativist model is immediately in trouble. It hinges on the view (not further defended) that the ordinary *second* person

---

[23] This view seems strengthened by A. Kaplan (82) and R. Carnap (19); cf., A. J. Ayer (195) and (6). Cf. B. Kuklick (89).

[24] "A word or sentence seems to be called 'descriptive' on account of the fact that it is *not* emotive, does *not* commend, does *not* entail an imperative, and so on according to the theory involved." Foot ((40); see (249), p. 12).

imperative is the clear case of action-guiding language, but it must now say that in moral decisions only a special self-addressed imperative is action-guiding in the required sense. And can the notion of a self-addressed command do the work the theory requires?[25]

I do not find the notion, or metaphor, of a self-addressed imperative wholly unintelligible. Moreover, Hare is not absurdly suggesting that I always do utter such an imperative to myself before acting; rather he claims to be elucidating the formal structure of practical reasoning. But is a self-addressed command the appropriate notion? The basic difficulty is that an ordinary command requires at least two people, giver and recipient, and several logical features of commands or imperatives do not carry over happily into the metaphorical situation.

Firstly a command normally presupposes authority. If we had no social structures which authorized one person to control another, we could have a mood of the verb which indicated a threat, a request, etc., but it could not have the full force of our imperative. But if authority is essential to a command, what is the analogy in a self-addressed one? Secondly it is always logically possible for an authority to be disobeyed. If I cannot disobey a self-addressed command, the metaphor becomes nonsense. If I can, then who is uttering the imperative and who is refusing to obey and which bit is "me"? Finally, what is the difference meant to be between my self-addressed command "Do X!" and my decision to do X? If there is none, if all this is just metaphorical talk about making up my mind, then what is to be gained by re-describing the process as if I were a polity or a tribunal? But if the talk is more than metaphorical, if it is meant to *throw light* on the process of choosing, surely it can do so only by taking seriously the parallel with ordinary commands, and thus raising the previous problems.

A better suggestion might be this. Though I may cease to ask the question "What shall I do?" for many reasons—e.g., because I go to sleep—yet surely what brings my deliberation to its proper end is not a command but a decision. Perhaps, then, we should treat remarks like "That would be cruel," not as disguised imperatives, but as reasons for or against a decision. What can count as a reason will be a large question for investigation, but it is implausible to suggest that

---

[25] Cf. Nowell-Smith, *Ethics* ((229), p. 191), J. Margolis (106). There is a parallel here with Russell's *Logical Atomism*. He started with a naming theory of meaning which assumed that proper names provide the perspicuous, unpuzzling case of how language connects with the world. He had to end by concluding that proper names are not logically proper names. In each case the later argument erodes its own starting point.

imperatives alone can be reasons which answer the question "What shall I do?"

This emphasis on reasons for decision might suit those anti-naturalists who refuse to collapse evaluation into prescription. Thus P. W. Taylor suggests that when a man is asking what he should do, then if we offer a value judgment we answer his question indirectly by giving him a reason for doing one thing rather than another, while if we prescribe one course we answer his question directly, but without giving him a reason ((248), p. 230). Yet Hare's position at least flows consistently from his view that only a command can answer the question "What shall I do?", and thus it preserves the principle that no statement of fact can be a reason for action. If we give it up, then the question "What is a reason for an action?" must be raised afresh. It has, of course, been raised by many.[26] But this is one of the places where the debate about naturalism in ethics depends on something else, in this case on philosophy of action.

3. "OUGHT"[27]

Hare declares his anti-naturalist allegiance to "Hume's Law (no 'ought' from an 'is')" (FR, p. 108).[28] On what is the "Law" based? It might seem to follow from a particular doctrine of inference, that a conclusion must in some sense be "contained in" the premises, coupled with the point that "ought" does not mean the same as "is" and hence cannot be contained in it. This view is one possible but highly debatable interpretation of Hume's own position.[29] In any case it is wrong. The gap between evaluation and description must be something that mere grammar may mask as well as reveal; since, e.g., "*X is* wrong" commits us to "*X ought* not to be done." Conversely, it is irrelevant for opponents to point out that *compound* moral pro-

---

[26] E.g., by Nowell-Smith in his account in terms of pro- and con- attitudes ((229), chap. 8). I have elsewhere commented on one aspect of his account ((211), chap. 12, sect. 3).

[27] For this section I am heavily indebted to W. D. Hudson's admirable anthology *The Is-Ought Question* (220). I omit "right," "duty," and "obligation," because they have been relatively little discussed in the last decade (though cf. e.g., J. K. Mish'alani (109), H. L. A. Hart (67)). Doubtless they belong to the same family as "ought," but I am not happy with the common assumption that they are virtually synonymous with it.

[28] For various relevant distinctions often neglected in this field, cf. D. Mitchell (111).

[29] I cannot enter into Humean exegesis. On this debate the following papers are collected in Hudson's volume: A. C. MacIntyre (97), R. F. Atkinson (5), G. Hunter (76), (77), A. G. N. Flew (37), W. D. Hudson (72). In addition, see M. J. Scott-Taggart (146), A. R. Konrad (87), D. Mitchell (110), B. T. Wilkins (186), R. J. Glossop (55), R. E. Creel (27), B. J. Diggs (29), N. Capaldi (18).

positions can be derived from purely factual premisses.[30] Even Hare allows (LM, pp. 34–36) that hypothetical imperatives can be derived from descriptive statements.

Presumably the basic principle is again that factual statements cannot entail action-guiding ones. Such words as "entail" and "analytic" are perhaps used too freely in the debate; but in this context a logical link exists between premisses p and conclusion q, if the fact that a man accepted p and denied q would lead us to say, not merely that he held very peculiar views, but that he could not mean by the words what we mean. Such points of meaning are to be decided by the wit and judgment of the philosopher speaking his native tongue. This must leave a penumbra of debatable cases, but where we have no sharp instrument we must be content with a blunt one.

A recurring distinction (which applies also to discussions of "good") is between the claim that "ought" *in general* cannot be derived from "is," and the claim that specifically *moral* "oughts" cannot. Formalist arguments from the nature of inference are clearly about "is" and "ought" in general, not about moral and non-moral. But some examples suggested that various "is's" imply "oughts" in a stronger sense than a mere translation of, say, "is wrong" into "ought not." E.g., from the fact that I have sold my house it surely follows that I *legally* ought to give up possession. Many anti-naturalists reply by appealing again to the thesis of autonomy, that at least *moral* principles and obligations are not entailed by any facts. But the thesis of moral autonomy can then gain no support from the general formalist arguments.

Naturalist attempts to derive "oughts" have two (not inconsistent) starting points: firstly *wants or needs*, and secondly *rules*. This division is of course a cross-classification from the distinction between moral and non-moral "oughts." There have been various appeals to wants or needs, of which perhaps the best known is Anscombe's functionalist account: " . . . machinery needs oil, or should or ought to be oiled, in that running without oil is bad for it, or it runs badly without oil."[31] Secondly as to derivations from rules, Max Black has argued

[30] E.g., "If A, then B" implies "If B ought not to be done, then A ought not to be done." Cf. A. N. Prior (136) (137), D. R. Kurtzman (91), M. Black ((13); see (220), pp. 100–102). G. W. Roberts (140), H. N. Castaneda (22) (21), P. H. Nowell-Smith and E. J. Lemmon (126).

[31] ((3); see (220), p. 179). Cf. also Nowell-Smith's *Ethics* (229), A. MacIntyre ((220), pp. 45–46), M. Zimmerman (188) (189); see (220), C. G. Werner (183). Zimmerman tries to eliminate "oughts" totally rather than to derive them, arguing that everything they say could be said by statements about our wants. The objections of W. D. Hudson ((220), pp. 19–21) and K. Hanly, ((60); see (220), p. 92) seem to me successful. In particular I would argue: (1) that Zimmerman assumes a

((13), see (220), p. 99) that certain factual statements about a chess game entail that a player should (or ought to) move the queen, and further that the same may hold in some moral cases.[32] But undoubtedly the most debated claim is J. R. Searle's "How to derive 'ought' from 'is'" ((147); see (220), p. 120). He claims ((220), p. 121) to move deductively from "Jones uttered the words 'I hereby promise to pay you, Smith, five dollars'" to "Jones ought to pay Smith five dollars," without employing any evaluative utterances in the process.[33]

Searle's thesis centers, I think, on his account of "institutional facts." There are utterances, such as that "*A* married *B*," which clearly state a fact; yet they presuppose certain institutions, without which the same observable acts could not amount to a marriage.[34] Searle argues in effect that to use institutional language, without explicit qualification or special circumstances, is to accept the institution. There is, in this broad sense, an institution of promising, and "I promise . . . " invokes it. This does not show that promise-keeping is a morally desirable institution (cf. (220), pp. 127, 132n). But unless one uses "promise" in an inverted commas sense etc. (cf. p. 128), to utter the words "I promise . . . " is to put oneself under an obligation.

Objections cluster into two types. The first is that Searle in various places uses a "*ceteris paribus*" or "other things being equal" clause in connecting his successive statements, and it is claimed that these involve, despite his denial, covert moral evaluations (e.g. (220), pp. 157, 163). On this point: (1) I think his critics have fastened on aspects of his exposition that are defective, but this does not seem fundamental to his position. Promising is a defeasible concept, (cf. (220), p. 122) and

pure and undefended ethical subjectivism (cf. (220), p. 85); and (2) that some of his "is's" are really as evaluative as "*X* is wrong"; cf., e.g., his use of "acceptable" ((220), p. 88). Werner's equally extreme position turns on the contention, not further defended, that to say "you ought to do *X*, even if it will make you unhappy," is "sheer effrontery" ((183), p. 136).

[32] For criticism see D. Z. Phillips ((134); see (220), p. 114). However, he seems to concede Black's thesis in the non-moral case ((220), p. 114). Thus (though cf. R. Montague (115)) the crucial issue is again that of moral autonomy. On this and related points see also G. P. Baker and P. M. Hacker (8), H. N. Castaneda (21) (22), M. F. Cohen (24).

[33] Cf. also Searle's later discussion in (243); see (220) at end. The following discussions of his paper are again collected in Hudson's volume (and see his comments pp. 24–26): A. G. N. Flew (38), R. M. Hare (65), J. E. McClellan and B. P. Komisar (95), J. and J. J. Thomson (177), W. D. Hudson (73). See also G. P. Baker and P. M. Hacker (8), N. Cooper (25), L. C. Holborow (69), A. Ralls (138), H. Schwyzer (145), R. Montague (113) (115), J. G. Gill (53), G. I. Mavrodes (108), E. K. Jobe (79), P. D. Shaw (153), K. Baier (7).

[34] It is here that the appeal lies to the concept of a rule, since the notion of an institution is further elucidated in terms of a distinction between regulative and constitutive rules ((220), p. 131).

sometimes to decide whether *A* promised is itself to make a debatable, normative, moral assessment. But sometimes not. There are clear cases where to utter "I promise . . . " is promising, just as there are clear cases (e.g., play acting) where it is not. The *ceteris paribus* merely allows for the borderlines. (2) Searle has in any case later argued ((243); cf. (220), p. 259) that the *ceteris paribus* can be dropped.[35]

The second type of objection (cf. (220), pp. 134, 144) is that Searle conflates fact-stating with commitment-undertaking. To say "He promised . . . " either states a fact, namely that he uttered certain words, *or* it claims that he undertook an obligation; but we must not confuse the two. A crucial issue here is whether the objection is to deriving any "ought" or only a moral one; an issue easily clouded because the particular example in fact involves a moral one. The objectors' concern seems for the most part specifically moral, and in effect to be again the issue of moral autonomy.[36] Thus Flew ((220), p. 139) takes Searle's view to be or to entail that if we say a man promised we are committed to morally endorsing the institution of promising. But this misses the point: Searle denies the commitment, and moral autonomy is not even in issue.

Assertions involving institutional facts seem often what we might call "defeasibly moral judgments."[37] They describe situations in a way which commits the speaker to moral judgments *unless* there is a qualification. Such language provides a vocabulary which makes it very easy to express, and very cumbersome to deny, moral relationships which would otherwise need elaborate circumlocutions. It has its dangers, but is also useful to the point of indispensibility.[38] "Unless's" are always possible—moral qualifications, inverted commas uses, etc.—which is why moral autonomy is not in issue. What is in issue is what Searle calls the classical empiricist picture of how words relate to the world ((220), pp. 128–130). If institutional facts are facts, and if they presuppose given social practices which may in turn

[35] H. Beran has put to me a further impressive suggestion. Perhaps "obligation" expresses *a* reason for doing something, while "ought" expresses a *conclusive*, all-things-considered reason (cf. n. 27). For we say a man has conflicting obligations (e.g., to his family and to his employer), but hardly that he ought to do each of two incompatible things. If so, then even if Searle has not derived an "ought" from an "is," he may still have derived a moral obligation; and this also would refute anti-naturalism.

[36] This is clearly the case with Flew ((38); see (220), pp. 136–138). I am not so sure about Hare ((65); see (220), pp. 152–155).

[37] The responsibility for the notion is mine. If Searle should wish to say he really made the point first, I should not quibble.

[38] Much explanation is needed here. For a discussion of some closely related issues see my (211), pp. 193–197. The controversy about Anscombe's grocer is also relevant. See Anscombe ((4); (249), p. 71), D. Z. Phillips (132) (133), C. Williamson (187).

presuppose evaluations, we again meet the question whether a sharp distinction between fact and value can be maintained (cf. Sect. 6).

* * *

All this does not give us an account of "ought." That account is in principle to be obtained, I believe, by a process of linguistic analysis, which may provide relevant material for, but does not itself depend upon, any theory such as prescriptivism or its rivals.[39] I have not done the analysis so I do not know the answer, but I am prepared to swap intuitions with Anscombe, Hare, and others.[40]

I suspect that the most general notion expressed by "ought" is that of acknowledging a restriction on possibilities of action. There are cases ("You ought to leave now if you want to catch the next bus") where only the situation restricts the possibilities—to go or miss the bus. Yet despite such cases we would have little use for "ought," I think, unless we tended to rank our wants and aims in hierarchies of acceptability. When we have policies or priorities, however arrived at, which are not considered to be up for revision with every passing whim, then above all we say we ought to do what they imply, despite the counter-considerations. Our policy or priority now commits us. This is the restriction (which of course does not remove our freedom to choose otherwise) that seems most typically expressed by an "ought."

This makes "ought" primarily a word for talking about certain human choices. When followed by a passive infinitive (" . . . ought to be X'd") it seems in effect a passive form of the verb, indicating that some obligation (etc.) exists in respect of the grammatical subject. Thus the Anscombean "Machinery ought to be oiled" indicates that we ought to oil machinery for *our* purposes, not that machinery itself has wants or needs. As for the Harean thesis that "ought" is prescriptive, it must stand or fall with prescriptivism in general.

[39] Many issues arise over an appeal to linguistic analysis: whether analysis of moral terms can be morally neutral; what cultural or other assumptions it may mask; whether any conclusions can be reached except by making distinctions between "central" and "peripheral" uses in a way which may beg important questions; what philosophical point there may be in showing how a moral term actually functions in our language and our society; and so on. But philosophers constantly make claims about what it means to say "You ought to . . . " and the like. Such claims, it would seem, must either be about what the relevant term ordinarily does mean, or else be recommendations about what it should mean; and even in the latter case we would surely do well to know what it does mean so as the better to assess the recommendation. If we want to know what it does mean, then a meticulous investigation of how it is actually used, sustained by a steady resolve to investigate the linguistic phenomena without prior commitment to a theory of how it must be used, seems the way to find out.

[40] Cf. also J. K. Mish'alani (109), J. Margolis (104), A. Sloman (157).

I repeat that I have not done the linguistic analysis required to defend my suggestions. What seems to me clear is that work of this sort needs to be done, and preferably not in order to support an already-held theory. Whether on my view we could derive an "ought" from an "is" would presumably depend on what is involved in ranking wants in hierarchies of acceptability, and what sorts of facts might be relevant, and how, to such a process.

4. "GOOD"[41]

The most impressive anti-naturalist account of the central, action-guiding meaning of "good" is to appeal to its Oxford English Dictionary definition as (*inter alia*) "the most general adjective of commendation.[42] Hare's usual terminology, for example, is that "good" has both prescriptive (commendatory) meaning and descriptive meaning (the features of the thing in virtue of which we call it good), but that the former is in some sense primary or fundamental.[43] Since the relevant "descriptive" features of the thing do not enter fundamentally into the meaning, "good" has no fixed descriptive content. Again the objection will arise that *sometimes* the descriptive content is undeniable; nothing could be a good knife unless it cuts efficiently. Again anti-naturalists must decide which way to go on this point. Again most fall back on the thesis of autonomy, and tend to deny fixed content for moral goodness only.[44] I too am here concerned only with "morally good."

[41] Since the Naturalistic Fallacy was formulated, and is chiefly discussed, in relation to "good," this seems the best place to list general discussions of it. Those specifically relating to Moore's version have been cited in Sect. 1, and those specifically relating to Hare are cited later in this section when I discuss his version of the Fallacy. See, in addition, K. Nielsen (125), G. Schrader (144), G. J. Stack (165), G. P. Baker and P. M. Hacker (8), L. O. Kattsoff (83), H. Margenau and F. Oscanyan (103), D. H. Monro (227), P. W. Taylor ((248), chap. 9), P. H. Nowell-Smith (229), pp. 36–43 (and on Nowell-Smith, Frankena ((44), see (226), pp. 47 *et seq*.). On the closely cognate question (or alternative formulation) concerning the relation of fact to value, see L. W. Sumner (172), G. W. Roberts (140), C. Beck (11), M. A. Slote (160), J. Fletcher (36), G. O. Allen (2).

[42] Commendation is taken to involve a justifiable preference. Thus in calling something good one does not offer, but one indicates that one can offer, a reason for approval.

[43] Cf LM, p. 117. His whole account contains difficulties which I cannot here discuss.

[44] Hare's considered view is, I think, that in the case of "functional" words (LM, p. 100); ((63), see (210), pp. 78–79) such as "knife," where the very meaning indicates what the thing is for, "good" has fixed descriptive meaning. His primary concern, though not always his argument, is for the principle of autonomy (cf. (210), pp. 81–82). By contrast I do not know what his position is about deducing non-moral oughts (cf. (65); see (220), pp. 152–155).

There are, I think, two major naturalist objections to this position, both stated forcefully by (*inter alia*) P. Foot. The first is that we cannot analyze moral discourse into a pure description plus an extra non-descriptive somewhat. E.g., *ad hominem* against Hare, the extra somewhat cannot be a self-addressed imperative, for

> I can speak of someone else as having the virtue of courage, and of course recognize it as a virtue in the proper sense, while knowing that I am a complete coward, and making no resolution to reform.[45]

The second objection is that this must make morality irrational and subjective, for it means that

> . . . a moral eccentric could argue to moral conclusions from quite idiosyncratic premisses. . . . He could also reject someone else's evaluation simply by denying that his evidence was evidence at all.[46]

A final assessment of these arguments must wait till Sects. 5 and 6. In this section I discuss only two important challenges to anti-naturalism, which I call the functionalist and the speech-act objections.[47]

Fundamentally, functionalism returns for inspiration to Aristotle.[48] To be good is to fulfill the proper function of a thing of that kind. More detailed formulations are so far lacking.[49] But it is at least clear that the paradigms in this approach to "good" are functional words like "knife." Foot has indeed pointed out ((220), pp. 217–218) that the notion applies in the case of more words than those which are functional in any normal sense of the word. But the crucial question is whether "good man" or "good action" in *moral* contexts can similarly be given a descriptive, functional meaning.[50] I make four comments.

[45] (41); see (210), p. 96.
[46] *Ibid.*, p. 84.
[47] For important accounts which I cannot discuss, cf. A. Sloman (156), F. E. Sparshott (245), R. S. Hartman (219). Apart from the content which functionalism aims to give to "good," there are interesting attempts to supply content by drawing on scientific (e.g., anthropological) evidence. I cite as examples only, Edel (*op. cit.*), J. Ladd (224).
[48] Its most distinguished exponents are in particular P. Foot, P. T. Geach, G. E. M. Anscombe. For other discussions of the ethical views of these three, see *inter alia*, Hare ((63), see (210)), A. Stigen (169), J. Teichmann (175), A. P. Griffiths and R. S. Peters (56), A. L. Thomas (176). On whether this functionalism represents the true Aristotle, cf. S. Hampshire (57).
[49] Foot claims that, at least for many cases, things are good if they are "of the kind to perform their function well" ((39); see (220), p. 226). This is not, I think, meant to apply universally. In any case the final "well," which seems essential, reduces the claim to the circular one that a thing is good if it performs its function goodly.
[50] In *the Philosophy of Language* (221) (cf. (84)). J. J. Katz outlines a position which distinguishes between use, function, duties, purposes, pleasurability, etc. as criteria of goodness (pp. 294–295). His view is broadly functionalist as I use the term. Since he expressly offers no account of "good man" (p. 311), his treatment

(1) Firstly there is, again, moral autonomy. Here it seems to me that functionalists, can indeed cross the moral border. Many moral judgments are based, in F. H. Bradley's phrase, on "my station and its duties"; and then "(morally) good" has for functional reasons a partly fixed content. To say (cf. Foot (220), pp. 218–219) that someone is a good daughter is a moral assessment, yet it would be unintelligible to say that she was a good daughter *because* she betrayed her parents to the secret police.[51] But this does not capture the anti-naturalist citadel. For a man may ask whether the duries which his role or function prescribes are, after all, his true moral obligation; e.g., whether his obligations as a good soldier conflict with his obligations as a good man. Morality has a "final court of appeal" aspect, to which talk of moral autonomy points; the question (cf. Sect. 5) is whether functionalism obscures it.

(2) Can one achieve a functional definition of "man" except by building into the definition some notion which is in effect evaluative — some non-empirical notion of what is the true or real function or nature of man? If not, the meaning which gives the fixed descriptive content itself involves a prior value-judgment, and hence gives a reason for choosing only if the questioner accepts the ideal. This challenge presents a burden of proof which functionalists have not, I think, discharged.[52]

(3) Insofar as functionalists base morality on wants or needs, they agree with Hare, who similarly starts from men's actual interests; and both contrast with anti-naturalists$_1$ who would base morality on intuition or the like. But functionalism further argues that if someone asks why he should do what is good, then in Geach's words, "the only relevant answer is an appeal to something the questioner *wants*" ((210), p. 70); cf. Anscombe ((220), pp. 181–182), Foot ((210), pp. 95–97). So a crucial moral issue (cf. Foot, *ibid.*) is the central question of Plato's *Republic*: how can we show that it pays a man to be just, in the way that it pays to be prudent, courageous or temperate? The argument aims to move from my immediate wants to my real needs,

---

seems only marginally relevant to ethics. On Katz cf. I. A. Snook (162), M. Ginsberg (54). For another functionalist position see Z. Vendler (179) and on Vendler see T. E. Patton and P. Ziff (130).

[51] It would be intelligible, even if outrageous, to say that she was thereby a good citizen. But again not anything could count as the act of a good citizen.

[52] Cf. on this issue Hare ((210), pp. 80–82), Hampshire, *Thought and Action* ((215), chap. 4), Margolis (105). Foot largely agrees with this, and modifies her account of "good" in consequence ((210), pp. 7–9). I think what I say later applies to her position too. I have presented the objection as telling against only this particular form of naturalism. Hare would no doubt think it generalizable against any form, but this leads to point (4).

appealing still to what really profits me. Hare's universalizability, on the other hand, takes wants or needs as the basis for formulating rules which are binding on me, not necessarily because they profit *me*, but because I judge them to be appropriate for *all* cases.

This conflict is in essence the Greeks *vs.* Kant all over again. Surely it must be a side issue; whether all justifications must refer to our *own* good cannot be the same question as whether "*X* is good" states a fact. But I cannot resist a very brief comment. That a man must have a pro- or con-attitude towards whatever he does may perhaps profitably be made a tautology;[53] but this does not mean that the only thing towards which he can have a pro-attitude is his own benefit. The latter view might be held as a matter of fact, as a matter of logic, or as a belief about what is rational conduct, but in all senses it seems false. As a matter of fact, a man who sacrifices himself for others may not consider anything but the benefit that *others* will receive. *Must* he then, as a matter of logic, have taken himself somehow to benefit? I see no reason why. Is it, then, possible to act purely for the good of others, but irrational to do so, because the only *good* reasons for actions are in terms of the agent's benefit? Again I see no reason to agree. Certainly the problem remains; how can we show a man he should be just, when he will ask only whether he will benefit? But in my view the task is not to answer his question but to persuade him to ask a different one: namely, what about other people? The persuasion is not only or perhaps chiefly a task for philosophers. But at least they need not hinder it by adopting a definition of "rational" that makes purely altruistic action irrational.[54]

(4) Finally there is Hare's general argument against any naturalism, which is his version of the Naturalistic Fallacy.[55] I shall first maintain that his argument as it stands begs the question, and then propound a somewhat similar argument which tells against naturalism but not in favor of prescriptivism.

Hare's contention is that a definition of "good" in terms of a

[53] Though perhaps not; see (211), pp. 245–248.

[54] Some naturalists (though not functionalists) would ask what empirical facts make it possible for other-regarding motives to move men. An answer might be that we are evolved from animals which had group-preserving as well as self-preserving instincts, and thus are creatures which *can* be moved by consideration for others. My point is that there is no good reason to dignify only self-regarding considerations with the word "rational."

[55] Cf. LM, pp. 83 *et seq.* For discussions of essentially Hare's version of the Fallacy see J. F. Lange (92), B. Kuklick (89), P. Kurtz (90), P. D. Shaw (153), L. W. Sumner (171), R. L. Holmes (70), J. B. Stearns (167) (166), J. W. Nickel (124), D. Mitchell (110), H. Veatch (178), C. Daniels (28), D. Lewis (94), R. Hancock (59), S. Stojanovic (170), E. M. Adams (190).

descriptive characteristic C will prevent us from using it to commend. After an example (LM, p. 84) which needs more discussion than I can give,[56] he goes on:

> Let us generalise. If 'P is a good picture' is held to mean the same as 'P is a picture and P is C', then it will become impossible to commend pictures for being C; it will be possible only to say that they are C.[57]

The soundness of this conclusion will depend *inter alia* on what commending is. Hare clearly requires a premiss that we cannot commend P by stating some fact about it, such as that it is C; i.e., that fact-stating or describing is totally different from commending or prescribing. But this is just what his opponents deny; they hold, presumably, that we commend something *by* stating certain facts about it, such as that it is good. So the argument begs the question against them.[58]

However I now wish to suggest a substitute argument which turns not on a descriptive/prescriptive dichotomy but on the nature of moral disagreement. Take two rival moral philosophers, such as a functionalist and an intuitionist. Suppose each gives "good" a fixed descriptive content, and thus makes his conception of human goodness part of his meaning of the word. Now surely the difference between them is purely verbal. They find that each uses the *sign* "good" with a different meaning, and what is left in dispute? "Everything is left in dispute," it might be replied. "For 'good' here refers to our ultimate human goals and forms of conduct, of which they give differing accounts." But "good" can refer to those matters only if those are what it refers to. This gives it some meaning such as "Those

---

[56] Because it switches crucially from "good picture" to "good taste."

[57] P. 85.

[58] I hope I have picked out the crucial element, though the argument has other puzzling features. The final clause ("it will be possible only to say that they are C") may hint at either of two further contentions. (1) Hare seems to suggest (cf. pp. 84 bottom, 154) that a factual definition C of "good" reduces "P is a good picture" to a tautology—apparently the tautology that "A picture which is C is C." I cannot see why. If I held, absurdly, that "good" meant "rectangular," this still would not reduce the synthetic "P is a good [i.e., rectangular] picture" to the analytic "A picture which is rectangular is rectangular." (2) He might have in mind the view (correct, as I believe) that "P is good" implies we can give reasons for approving it, and might hold that on any naturalist definition the remark "P is good because it is C" will reduce to the triviality that "P is C because it is C." Well certainly, if we have *already agreed* that " 'X' means 'ABC,' " then if we say "P is X because it is ABC," the "because" may be trivial or vacuous. But a naturalist could still treat "P is good because it is ABC" as non-trivial in several ways according to context: either (a) making a claim (if the definition were not previously agreed) about the meaning of "good"; or (b) giving the information that P is in fact good, because he has just discovered it is ABC; or perhaps (c) commending P by stating that it was good [i.e., ABC].

F

goals etc., *whatever they may be*, which we should adopt"; and this has no fixed descriptive content in the relevant sense. Though I *can* use "good" so that my standards are good by definition, I cannot then consistently use it to indicate that they are to be preferred to yours; e.g., "Mine are good and yours are not" reduces to "Mine are different to yours, and I use the sign 'good' to refer to mine." We must then find another sign without fixed descriptive content—e.g., "preferable" —before we can engage in moral debate.[59]

This argument is obviously reminiscent of Hare's. But it rests only on the desirability of keeping the meaning of the most general moral term, "good," neutral as between rival accounts of what is good, and thus lacking fixed descriptive content. It does not require anti-naturalism and is compatible with the view that "*X* is good" states some sort of high-level fact.[60]

*   *   *

The other criticism of anti-naturalism which I shall discuss is what Searle (*Speech Acts*, (243), pp. 136–139) calls "Speech act analyses," of the form "The word *W* is used to perform speech act *A*." He attributes to Hare the analysis that "the word 'good' is used to commend." This is certainly another area where ethics passes into something else, namely philosophy of language. I shall have to begin where most people do, with Austin's threefold classification into locutionary, illocutionary and perlocutionary acts (see (193)). This in turn presupposes the distinction between language and speech; where language is, roughly, a group's shared device for communication, and speech is the activity of using this device. The locutionary act belongs to language, and consists of uttering some meaningful words. The other two belong to speech; illocutionary acts are what one may do in

[59] Though I have followed the distinguished Moorean/Harean precedent of rejecting naturalism in a few lines, I realize this is a sketch of an argument which requires vast elaboration. E.g., (1) in fact "good" can be, and is, used with a gradation of meanings from the purely descriptive through the defeasibly moral to the descriptively neutral. I am only arguing that we need the latter use in ethics. E.g. (2) "Can't we agree ostensively on a list of good actions, ideals, etc. and proceed to discover by rational reflection what they have in common? Then can't we report this by saying '*A*, *B*, and *C* are really good'?" Yes we can, and normative ethics often does. But if it states its results by making *A*, *B*, and *C* part of the meaning of "good" instead of the things it claims to be good, it can have only a trivial verbal victory over any rival.

[60] Compare the claim of axiology that its insistence on the "emptiness" of the notion of "good" avoids the Naturalistic Fallacy. Cf. R. S. Hartman (68), p. 98, (219); N. Rescher (236), chap. 5. There is also a connection with W. V. Quine's notion of "semantic ascent" in so far as it is a "strategy . . . of ascending to a common part of two fundamentally disparate conceptual schemes, the better to discuss the disparate foundations" ((235), p. 272).

uttering words, such as warning or describing, and "perlocutionary" refers to casual consequences, such as frightening or enlightening.

The core of the objection is that commending is an illocutionary act, something we do in uttering certain words.[61] Hence, it is argued: (a) commending, being an illocutionary act, is attributable to sentences rather than to words like "good"; (b) it is attributable to "speech," while word-meaning is a matter of "language"; (c) the illocutionary force of commendation is neither necessary nor sufficient in the occurrence of a word like "good." Here I can discuss only the central point of Searle's argument. It is a necessary condition for a successful speech act analysis that the word mean the same in all grammatical contexts. "Good" fails this test. For, Searle says:

> "If this is good, then we ought to buy it", is not equivalent to "if I commend this, then we ought to buy it". "This used to be good" is not equivalent to "I used to commend this". "I wonder whether this is good" is not equivalent to "I wonder whether I commend this," etc.,[62]

I think the argument shows conclusively "this is good" does not mean "I commend this." Yet it still seems possible to paraphrase each example in terms of a remark about commendation which seems to capture the essential force of "good." But all such paraphrases must be *gerundive*, using such forms as "commendable," "worthy of commendation," etc. (e.g., "If this is worthy of commendation, then we ought to buy it.") The argument does not show that "good" cannot be defined in terms of what we might call commendability. Yet such a suggestion it seems, would displease everyone. On the one hand, "good" on this view lacks fixed descriptive content, and would therefore be rejected by functionalists and most other naturalists. On the other hand, "*X* is good" would now assert that *X has* certain characteristics, namely those that make it commendable, and thus, contrary to anti-naturalism, would surely be a proposition.[63]

The most important implication of the principle that commendation is an illocutionary force relates to the basic anti-naturalist dichotomy of fact and value. Clearly a sentence may have more than one illocutionary force; i.e., we may be doing more than one thing in uttering it.

---

[61] The best starting point is Urmson's lucid and temperate discussion ((250), chap. 11), which considers a formulation of the argument by Searle (148) which is prior to *Speech Acts*, and also some parallel points made by Ziff (255). For an earlier discussion see R. Brandt ((200), esp. pp. 179–180, chap. 9). See also A. Sloman (158), A. Montefiore (117), Hare (64) R. Montague (114).

[62] P. 139.

[63] Hare, when arguing against Geach, once said that "good" means "roughly . . . 'having the characteristic qualities (whatever they are) which are commend-*able* in the kind of object in question'" ((210), p. 79, my emphasis). For reasons given this seems to conflict with his usual position.

Might we be both evaluating and stating? I make brief comments on four relevant illocutionary acts: stating a fact; describing (or ascribing a property); approving; commending.

Fact-stating seems to me a very broad category. Describing, and ascribing a property, are probably sub-classes; to describe something, etc. is to state a fact, but not necessarily *vice versa*. "There is no significant correlation between apple eating and lung cancer" hopefully states a fact, but surely it does not describe anything—not even non-existing significant correlations—nor does it ascribe a property. If so, then when a dichotomy between fact and value is assimilated to one between description (or property ascription) and evaluation (or prescription), there is already confusion on the left hand side of the distinction.[64]

Approving seems outside the category of fact-stating, and surely has some logical link with choice.[65] We may approve something without choosing or being willing to choose it, but we would not have the notion if we were not typically prepared to choose what we approved. I suspect that in its relevant sense "commend" involves both fact-stating and approving. Typically one commends something by stating facts about it, but facts picked out primarily for the purpose not of giving information but of showing that approval is justified.[66] Since approving has logical links with choice, commendation is typically action-guiding because it is linked with choosing at two removes.[67]

In short, as against anti-naturalism, that "*X* is good" must be action-guiding does not seem to entail that it cannot state a fact. As against naturalism, any account which gives "good" a fixed descriptive content must be squared with the need for a use which is neutral between rival accounts of what is good. I do not know what "good" means, nor whether there is, as there seems intuitively to be, a single thread of meaning through most of its uses. But an account which might cope with many difficulties is one in terms of commendability; perhaps that "*X* is good" typically means something like, "*X* has those characteristics which make it commendable in accordance with criteria which the speaker does not, but could, mention."

[64] I also believe (cf. Sect. 6) there is confusion to the right hand side.

[65] When the criteria for approval are known one can infer from the approval that certain facts are the case, but that does not make those facts part of the meaning.

[66] Hence the impressive naturalist point that commending cannot be an extra somewhat—let alone an extra imperative—stuck on to some bit of description.

[67] This reinforces my doubts about Hare's version of the Naturalistic Fallacy. Why can we not commend something by stating that it has the qualities which make it commendable?

5. MORAL REASONING AND MORAL AUTONOMY

Behind these meta-ethical issues lie others which at least are thought to depend on them. In particular: (1) is morality objective or subjective? (2) what about moral autonomy? On (1) I think both sides are right in being opposed to sheer subjectivism.[68] The relevant area of debate is that naturalists accuse anti-naturalists like Hare of being covert subjectivists despite such notions as universalizability, while anti-naturalists retort that to go further is to destroy moral autonomy. Thus (1) and (2) are linked.

Many have argued that universalizability is not enough. "What is put in issue is simply consistency"; if morality has no content, then "the choice of one general rule rather than another is still an arbitrary matter."[69] The objection seems borne out by Hare's own difficulty with what he calls the moral fanatic. Ordinary moral arguments, he says, consider other people's interests equally with one's own, but there are arguments based on ideals of human excellence (FR, chap. 7 and esp. pp. 138–139, 147, 149). The problem is that if a fanatic (e.g., a Nazi) says that his ideal (e.g., the purity of the Master Race) is important enough to override the interests of other people (e.g., Jews), then provided he admits that if he were Jewish he should himself be sent to the gas chambers, his position seems universalizable.

I would like to suggest, but not develop, the possibility that universalizability may have more power than Hare thinks.[70] I would use universalizability as a dialectical weapon, in the Socratic sense that it presupposes an interlocutor and takes as its starting point something he says. An act can be universalizable only *qua* act of such and such a type, i.e., under a particular description. A man must not only produce an internally consistent set of descriptions, but must also say what he thinks, and why, about competing descriptions offered by others. He may draw distinctions wherever he wishes, yet unless he

[68] Cf. Urmson (250), and in particular his discussion of "attitudes."

[69] G. Warnock (252), p. 43, R. S. Downie and E. Telfer (203), p. 124. Cf. also G. C. Kerner (86), B. Blanshard (199), pp. 254–255, G. W. Roberts (140) (141), G. Madell (102), J. C. Mackenzie (99), C. C. W. Taylor (173), H. J. White (184), T. M. Reed (139), B. Rosen (142), A. Ryan (143), R. Montague (116), R. Brandt (14), R. L. Holmes (70), G. Ezorsky (33).

[70] My points if correct to other authors, e.g., to what P. Edwards ((cf. 209), chap. 8) calls "fundamental moral judgments." Other philosophers have defended versions of universalizability, notably M. G. Singer (244) and A. Gewirth (esp. (52), (51)); cf. also R. Firth (35) and D. P. Gauthier (212). There is a large literature about which I make only two remarks. (1) The method of reasoning I describe seems closest to some aspects of G. E. Hughes' position (74). (2) I am not offering an account of moral reasoning, but of an aspect of it.

simply gives up arguing he must face questions and either provide consistent answers or modify his position. A dialectical dispute of this sort is exceedingly difficult to set out. Each question allows an indefinite number of alternative answers, each producing sub-alternatives, leading to sub- sub-alternatives. . . . But it is still a rational procedure.

Suppose we ask a hypothetical Nazi, "Why does your ideal entitle you to override other people's interests?" He must either (a) give reasons, or (b) refuse. If (b), he contracts out of reasoning altogether. If (a), are his convictions to be justified by their truth or by his mere sincerity? If by truth (i.e., by claims that Jews are in fact specially inferior, depraved, etc.) he commits himself to factual issues by which his position stands or falls; and it falls.[71] If by mere sincerity, then can *any* sincere fanatic—e.g., a devout super-Zionist—equally override the interests of, e.g., Nazis? If so, his position is not fanaticism at all, but an approval of total all-in conflict between different ideals. Why espouse this extreme moral *laissez-faire*? Perhaps he believes the best ideal will win? Again, then, is it enough that he *believes* it, or does he need evidence and if so what?

Or perhaps what justifies his position is its correctness, not his mere sincerity, but the only and sufficient reason for its correctness is the obvious glory of his ideal. Then is just seeming obvious a good enough reason *in general* for truth, or not? If no, then what is the relevant difference in his case? If yes, he is in no better position than the super-Zionist, and we end with moral *laissez-faire* again.

Perhaps the point is this. The fanatic really wishes to make an exception in his own favor. But he cannot rationally do this in morals any more than in science. He can claim the right to override others' interests only either by granting (and defending) an equal right to override his, or else by establishing a relevant difference—i.e., by giving *reasons* why his ideal alone is worthwhile. Incidentally the *actual* fanatic (who will almost never reason carefully anyway) usually slides from the "truth" defense to the "sincerity" defense and back again, depending on how the argument presses him.

These neo-Harean suggestions give no support to a logical framework of descriptive and prescriptive meaning. The argument is ultimately based on the claim, not that evaluative words are universalizable in virtue of their descriptive meaning, but that a good reason must (with qualifications I have not mentioned) be a good reason for anyone. Nor, incidentally, do I suggest that moral reasoning always

[71] The truth of his claim would of course be only a necessary condition. A justification of genocide would also need other (universalizable) principles, e.g., about the right of any superior race to eliminate any inferior one.

proceeds in this way. I only suggest that to minimize the power of universalizability by saying "what is put in issue is simply consistency," is to confuse a cheap consistency before cross-examination with a consistency dearly bought by meeting objections. Not merely the fanatic but the moral eccentric mentioned by Foot might find the price of the latter consistency beyond his means. He may certainly be asked whether he allows any other equally idiosyncratic concept of a good man; if so will he really accept the implications, and if not what grounds has he to back his own? I thus suggest that an anti-naturalist ethics need be less subjectivist than naturalists fear.

*　*　*

I turn to the second issue, moral autonomy. Perhaps some philosophers have thought that autonomy entails the view that moral issues are ultimately subjective.[72] The argument above suggests they may be wrong. In any case, what do anti-naturalists claim that they alone can preserve, and do their opponents violate it?[73]

Autonomy might be, or be confused with, the principle that only I can make my decisions. But this is a triviality which no naturalist denies. I think the thesis is a more substantial one about *moral* choice; that no authority whatever can remove the individual's ultimate moral responsibility to decide for himself what is right or wrong. Anti-naturalists have usually presented it as a doctrine about words. I think that such words as "good" (in "final court of appeal" contexts) do indeed lack the fixed descriptive content that naturalists have sought. But I also think anti-naturalists are not really making a linguistic point at all. For the linguistic investigation could have reached a different conclusion, and even now might do so;[74] and this would show only, in their view, that our current moral vocabulary needed drastic revision. That is why defeasibly moral obligations are compatible with autonomy.

Autonomy seems to me a normative moral claim with at least two aspects. Firstly it is a charter of freedom for the man who stands alone for conscience's sake. Secondly it is not only about freedom but also responsibility; that obeying orders, or accepting an authority blindly, is not a defense. As normative morals it may be challenged, or be subject to qualifications about whether obeying orders, for example,

---

[72] This may be the view of D. Z. Phillips and H. O. Mounce ((135); see (220), pp. 228, 235, 239); though whether they argue from autonomy to subjectivity or *vice versa* or both are issues needing more space than I have.

[73] Cf. T. D. Perry (131), A. Montefiore (117), A. P. Griffiths and R. S. Peters (56)

[74] It would be surprising, but by no means inconceivable, if so important a claim had been arrived at with *no* basis in our language.

may count at least as an extenuation. My question is whether there is any conflict between naturalists and anti-naturalists on the point.

I would really like to pose to naturalists this question rather than to answer it. I do not think they have offered any repudiation of autonomy;[75] but also I am not sure they accept it. They, too, have usually presented their argument as about the meaning of moral terms. I do hope they will say explicitly whether or not they hold that a fixed descriptive meaning of "good," etc., would, or is intended to, deprive men of the vocabulary in which they could make an autonomous decision.

Each side here detects in the other a certain arbitrariness or irrationality. Anti-naturalists reject, in the name of autonomy, what seems to them a way of telling a man that the current, or the "correct," moral vocabulary does not even allow him to state his view. Naturalists reject the view that a man can adopt any position as a moral one, provided he universalizes it with a lunatic consistency. Anti-naturalists deny that a man can be morally coerced by a group's linguistic fiat, while naturalists deny that he can escape censure by his own fiat. I have sufficient sympathy for each denial to hope that some ethical theory, whether or not it be like my neo-Harean one, might do justice to both.

6. Words and the World: A Conceptual Revolution?

In the whole fight there has been no knock-out, and I would hate to say who wins on points. On "ought" I incline against anti-naturalists; on "good" and on possible moral objectivity I suggest a view probably more pleasing to them than to their opponents; on moral autonomy naturalists also have some explaining to do. But I have criticized the whole theory of a fact/value dichotomy underlying anti-naturalism, and I end with some exploratory suggestions which underline that criticism. Perhaps they favor naturalism or perhaps they might transform the whole debate. The three most suggestive writers I have seen on these points are Searle, Anscombe and J. Kovesi.[76]

Searle ((243), Sect. 2.7: (220), pp. 128 et seq.) develops his contrast between "brute" and "institutional" facts till he challenges what he calls the basic empiricist picture of how words relate to the world. Anscombe ((4) cf. (3)) discusses a similar point in connection with

---

[75] Unless it be Anscombe's rejection of the moral "ought" as a "word of mere mesmeric force" ((3); see (220), p. 182).

[76] I have benefitted greatly from correspondence with Kovesi. Cf. also G. J. Stack (165), M. A. Slote (160), T. M. Olshewsky (129), P. T. Mackenzie (100), P.P. Nicholson (122).

possible dealings with her grocer, suggesting that if we look again at how we apply concepts to situations, then the notion of observing a single level of brute fact is totally misconceived.[77] Kovesi's *Moral Notions* (223) shows to my mind conclusively how subtle and various are the ways in which we apply concepts to what we observe. In general, protagonists in the debate about naturalism (especially anti-naturalists) take is-statements to be what report, or can be reduced to, brute observable facts. The problem has then been whether or how such unobservable things as values could possibly be linked to these facts. This whole way of thinking is now challenged.

This is more than the point, well established in philosophy of science and elsewhere, that our statements may be more or less theory-impregnated. For scientific remarks are commonly taken to be established by observations of brute facts (e.g., pointer readings). The new challenge is: are there brute facts? That I order potatoes from the grocer and he delivers them, are brute facts relative to the fact that I owe him money. That I utter words in his hearing is brute, relative to the fact that I ordered the potatoes. That certain sounds were emitted might be brute, relative to the fact that I uttered words. At the other end, that I owe him money may be brute, relative to whether I am solvent.

We think of the realm of fact as that of common sense or scientific observation. But what do I really observe? A housewife ordering potatoes? A human organism uttering certain sounds? The occurrence of certain sound waves (so that it takes science to tell me what I really observe)? And if we give, say, the third answer, how do we get from the sound waves to the placing of an order? If by an inference, then of what sort? If not, then is it by evaluating or assessing the observed data? But that would make the line between fact and evaluation relative to a context, so that a fact in one context would be an evaluation in another.

As for the role of inference: if we are to make rational connections between propositions, must they not be deductive or inductive? Then what is the connection between "She uttered certain sounds," and "She ordered some potatoes?" Do we add some premiss, or merely redescribe the same situation? We may have to re-examine here something not new but under-investigated. One species of the genus might be the Kantian notion of bringing representations under concepts, and another the Aristotelian one of seeing the universal in the particular. If we want a name for the genus, we might call it the process of *seeing that a concept applies to a situation*. Perhaps to do this is not a

---

[77] The implications for "defeasibly moral" judgments are not here relevant.

logical (deductive or inductive) process, nor an illogical one, but pre-logical; for unless we could do it we could not utter propositions and so could not have logical connections. So perhaps we do not move by inference from "is" to "ought," but simply recognize situations as cases to which ought-judgments apply. This I take to be one point of Kovesi's provocative paradox that "moral notions do not evaluate the world of description but describe the world of evaluation."[78]

A final problem, at least partly independent of these sweeping speculations but tending to reinforce them, is the relation of values and evaluations.[79] Talk of values, I would assume, ultimately either expresses, or states facts about, what men *approve*. But evaluation, I think, is not approving but assessing something as coming up to a standard. Where a standard is clearly fixed one may evaluate or assess without either expressing, or stating facts about, the values which presumably lie behind the standards. The apple sorter may not approve or even know the point of the standards he applies. Hence the assumption that evaluation is closely tied to value may often hold, if at all, only for an extended sense of "value." To apply *any* normal word—to decide whether an object is an antique or whether an action is cruel—is to assess according to a standard which the meaning of the word supplies. Hence, whatever we ultimately say about values, evaluation, so far from being a subjective coating on a slab of brute fact, seems inextricably involved in any linguistic activity, including that of stating a fact. If so, then unless we could, improbably, drive a wedge between value and evaluation to replace the old one between value and fact, the sharp dichotomy would disappear.

If this general approach should prevail, the "fact/value distinction" would vanish into an array of distinctions about the different ways that concepts apply to situations. Some issues I have discussed—e.g., the thesis of autonomy—might remain unscathed, but not many. That an "ought" could or could not be derived from an "is"; that if it could not, our values must be subjective, and that if it could, we would have no autonomy; that value and fact, prescription and description, action-guiding and fact-stating, are worlds apart; all these claims and more would be answered or reformulated, while vast new problems would arise. I would not be surprised or sorry if this happened. I

---

[78] (223), p. 119, cf. p. 161. My phrase "simply recognize" might have an un-intended intuitionist flavor, which could be avoided only by elucidating a whole set of distinctions.

[79] I owe this point to as yet unpublished work by Kovesi. He is not responsible for what I make of it.

would only hope that philosophers would not, in the pride of new discovery, ignore important issues in the debates we have known.[80]

University of New England

BIBLIOGRAPHY

With few exceptions I list only items mentioned in the text. They are cited there by their number in the bibliography (enclosed in parentheses). I cross-reference reprinted articles to the anthology, and give page references to the latter. E.g., if item (13) is reprinted in item (220), a typical page reference would be: ((13); see (220), p. 101).

A. ARTICLES

I use the following abbreviations.

APQ	*American Philosophical Quarterly*
An	*Analysis*
AJP	*Australasian Journal of Philosophy*
Dl	*Dialogue*
Dg	*Diogenes*
Eth	*Ethics*
IPQ	*International Philosophical Quarterly*
Iq	*Inquiry*
JP	*The Journal of Philosophy*
JVI	*Journal of Value Inquiry*
Kn	*Kinesis*
Mi	*Mind*
Mo	*Monist*
NS	*New Scholasticism*
No	*Nous*
PF	*The Philosophy Forum*
PQ	*Philosophical Quarterly*
PR	*The Philosophical Review*

[80] I owe a great deal to all members of the New England philosophy department. Two fragments of this survey which were read at staff seminars were faithfully torn to pieces and ultimately remoulded into far less objectionable form. For individual assistance I must, at the risk of invidious discrimination, particularly thank E. B. Robinson, B. C. Birchall and especially H. Beran. I am also indebted to P. H. Lucich and U. S. Pandey of the Sociology Department for references to literature in the social sciences.

PS   *Philosophical Studies* (University of Minnesota)
Ph   *Philosophy*
PPR   *Philosophy and Phenomenological Research*
PAS   *Proceedings of the Aristotelian Society*
PASS   *Proceedings of the Aristotelian Society* (Supplementary Volume)
PBA   *Proceedings of the British Academy*
Rt   *Ratio*
RIP   *Revue Internationale de Philosophie*
RM   *The Review of Metaphysics*
SJP   *Southern Journal of Philosophy*
Th   *Theoria*
Tm   *The Thomist*
UCS   *University of Colorado Studies* (Philosophy)

* * *

1. AIKEN, H. D. "The Concept of Moral Objectivity." See (201).
2. ALLEN, G. O. "From the 'Naturalistic Fallacy' to the Ideal Observer Theory," *PPR* vol. 30 (1969–70), 533.
3. ANSCOMBE, G. E. M. "Modern Moral Philosophy," *Ph* vol. 33 (1958). See (220), (249).
4. —— "On Brute Facts," *An* vol. 18 (1958), 69. See (249).
5. ATKINSON, R. F. "Hume on 'Is' and 'Ought': A Reply to Mr. Macintyre," *PR* vol. 70 (1961), 231. See (220).
6. AYER, A. J. "On the Analysis of Moral Judgments." See (196).
7. BAIER, K. "Moral Obligation," *APQ* vol. 3 (1966), 210.
8. BAKER, G. P. and HACKER, P. M. "Rules, Definitions and the Naturalistic Fallacy," *APQ* vol. 3 (1966), 299.
9. BAUMRIN, B. H. "Is there a Naturalistic Fallacy?" *APQ* vol. 5 (1968), 79.
10. BAYLIS, C. A. "C. I. Lewis's Theory of Value and Ethics," *JP* vol. 61 (1964), 559.
11. BECK, C. "Utterances which Incorporate a Value Statement," *APQ* vol. 4 (1967), 192.
12. BERGMANN, G. "Meaning and Ontology (Pt. II)," *Iq* vol. 5 (1962), 116, 129.
13. BLACK, M. "The Gap Between 'Is' and 'Should,' " *PR* vol. 73 (1964), 165. See (220).
14. BRANDT, R. Review of R. M. Hare's *Freedom and Reason*, *JP* vol. 61 (1964), 139.
15. BROAD, C. D. "G. E. Moore's Latest Published Views on Ethics," *Mi* vol. 70 (1961), 435.

16. BRUNTON, J. A. "Restrictive Moralities," *Ph* vol. 41 (1966), 113.
17. BURTT, E. A. "The Core of Dewey's Way of Thinking," *JP* vol. 57 (1960), 401.
18. CAPALDI, N. "Hume's Rejection of 'Ought' as a Moral Category," *JP* vol. 63 (1966), 126.
19. CARNAP, R. "Abraham Kaplan on Value Judgments." See (242).
20. CASTANEDA, H. N. "Ethics and Logic: Stevensonian Emotivism Revisited," *JP* vol. 64 (1967), 671.
21. —— "Imperatives, Decisions and 'Oughts': A Logico-Metaphysical Investigation." See (201).
22. —— "Imperatives, Oughts and Moral Oughts," *AJP* vol. 4 (1966), 277.
23. —— " 'Ought' and Assumption in Moral Philosophy," *JP* vol. 57 (1960), 791.
24. COHEN, M. F. " 'Is' and 'Should': An Unbridged Gap," *PR* vol. 74 (1965), 220.
25. COOPER, N. "Two Concepts of Morality," *Ph* vol. 41 (1966), 19.
26. COX, H. H. "Warnock on Moore," *Mi* vol. 79 (1970), 265.
27. CREEL, R. E. "The 'Is-Ought' Controversy," *Kn* vol. 1 (1969), 107.
28. DANIELS, C. "Hare on the Meaning of Good," *Mi* vol. 79 (1970), 139.
29. DIGGS, B. J. "A Technical Ought," *Mi* vol. 69 (1960), 301.
30. DUNCAN, E. H. "Has Anyone Committed the Naturalistic Fallacy?" *SJP* vol. 8 (1970), 49.
31. DURRANT, R. G. "Identity of Properties and the Definition of 'Good,' " *AJP* vol. 48 (1970), 360.
32. EAMES, S. M. "The Cognitive and the Non-Cognitive in Dewey's Theory of Valuation," *JP* vol. 58 (1961), 179.
33. EZORSKY, G. "*Ad Hominem* Morality," *JP* vol. 63 (1966), 120.
34. FALK, W. D. "Morality, Self and Others." See (201), (249).
35. FIRTH, R. "Ethical Absolutism and the Ideal Observer," *PPR* vol. 12 (1951–2), 414.
36. FLETCHER, J. "Virtue is a Predicate," *Mo* vol. 54 (1970), 66.
37. FLEW, A. G. N. "On the Interpretation of Hume," *Ph* vol. 38 (1963), 178. See (220).
38. —— "On Not Deriving 'Ought' from 'Is'," *An* vol. 25 (1964–5), 25. See (220).
39. FOOT, P. "Goodness and Choice," *PASS* vol. 35 (1961), 45. See (220).
40. ——"Moral Arguments," *Mi* vol. 67 (1958), 502. See (249).

41. FOOT, P. "Moral Beliefs," *PAS* vol. 59 (1958–9), 83. See (210), (220), (249).
42. FRANKENA, W. K. "C. I. Lewis on the Ground and Nature of the Right," *JP* vol. 61 (1964), 489.
43. —— "The Naturalistic Fallacy," *Mi* vol. 48 (1939), 464. See (210).
44. —— "Obligation and Motivation." See (226).
45. —— "Recent Conceptions of Morality." See (201).
46. FRANKS, G. "George Edward Moore's Criticism of some Ethical Theories," *Tm* vol. 31 (1967), 259.
47. —— "Was G. E. Moore Mistaken About Brentano?" *NS* vol. 43 (1969), 252.
48. GARVER, J. N. "On the Rationality of Persuading," *Mi* vol. 69 (1960), 163.
49. GAUTHIER, D. P. "Moore's Naturalistic Fallacy," *APQ* vol. 4 (1967), 315.
50. GEACH, P. T. "Good and Evil," *An* vol. 17 (1956), 33. See (210).
51. GEWIRTH, A. "Categorial Consistency in Ethics," *PQ* vol. 17 (1967), 289.
52. —— "The Generalization Principle," *PR* vol. 73 (1964), 229.
53. GILL, J. G. "An Abstract Definition of the Good," *Eth* vol. 80 (1969–70), 112.
54. GINSBERG, M. "Katz on Semantic Theory and 'Good'," *JP* vol. 63 (1966), 517.
55. GLOSSOP, R. J. "The Nature of Hume's Ethics," *PPR* vol. 27 (1966–7), 527.
56. GRIFFITHS, A. P. and PETERS, R. S. "The Autonomy of Prudence" *Mi* vol. 71 (1962), 161.
57. HAMPSHIRE, S. "Ethics: A Defense of Aristotle" *UCS* vol. 3 (1967).
58. HANCOCK, R. "A Note on Naturalism," *Eth* vol. 77 (1966–7), 62.
59. —— "The Refutation of Naturalism in Moore and Hare," *JP* vol. 57 (1960), 326.
60. HANLY, K. "Zimmerman's 'is-is': A Schizophrenic Monism," *Mi* vol. 73 (1964), 443. See (220).
61. HANNAFORD, R. V. " 'Exiting' from Moral Language," *JVI* vol. 4 (1970), 17.
62. HARE, R. M. "Descriptivism," *PBA* vol. 49 (1963), 115. See (220).
63. —— "Geach: Good and Evil," *An* vol. 18 (1957), 103. See (210).

64. HARE, R. M. "Meaning and Speech Acts," *PR* vol. 79 (1970), 3.
65. —— "The Promising Game," *RIP* vol. 70 (1964), 398. See (210), (220).
66. —— "Some Alleged Differences Between Imperatives and Indicatives," *Mi* vol. 76 (1967), 309.
67. HART, H. L. A. "Legal and Moral Obligation." See (226).
68 HARTMAN, R. S. "Sparshott's 'Enquiry into Goodness,'" *PPR* vol. 29 (1968), 97.
69 HOLBOROW, L. C. "Promising, Prescribing and Playing-Along," *Ph* vol. 44 (1969), 149.
70. HOLMES, R. L. "Descriptivism, Supervenience and Universalizability," *JP* vol. 63 (1966), 113.
71. HUBBELING, H. G. "The Logic of Criteria in Ethics and Philosophy of Religion," *Mi* vol. 79 (1970), 58.
72. HUDSON, W. D. "Hume on *Is* and *Ought*," *PQ* vol. 14 (1964), 246. See (220).
73. —— "The 'Is-Ought' Controversy," *An* vol. 25 (1964–5), 191. See (220).
74. HUGHES, G. E. "Moral Condemnation." See (226).
75. HUMBERT, E. R. "The 'Ought' and the 'Is'," *Mi* vol. 72 (1963), 581.
76. HUNTER, G. "Hume on *Is* and *Ought*," *Ph* vol. 37 (1962). See (220).
77. —— "A Reply to Professor Flew," *Ph* vol. 38 (1963), 182. See (220).
78. IRVING, J. A. "Comments," *JP* vol. 57 (1960), 442.
79. JOBE, E. K. "On Deriving 'Ought' from 'Is,'" *An* vol. 25 (1964–5), 179.
80. JOHNSON, J. P. "The Axiological Theism of Wilbur Marshall Urban," *IPQ* vol. 5 (1965), 335.
81. —— "The Fact-Value Question in Early Modern Value Theory," *JVI* vol. I (1967), 64.
82. KAPLAN, A. "Logical Empiricism and Value Judgments." See (242).
83. KATTSOFF, L. O. "The Discernment of Moral Qualities," *PPR* vol. 29 (1968), 68.
84. KATZ, J. J. "Semantic Theory and the Meaning of 'Good'," *JP* vol. 61 (1964), 739.
85. KENNEDY, G. "Comments," *JP* vol. 57 (1960), 436.
86. KERNER, G. C. "Approval, Reasons and Moral Argument," *Mi* vol. 71 (1962), 474.
87. KONRAD, A. R. "There is No 'Fact-Value Gap' for Hume," *JVI* vol. 4 (1970), 126.

88. KRIKORIAN, Y. H. "Cohen's Rationalistic Naturalism," *PPR* vol. 29 (1968), 264.

89. KUKLICK, B. "The Analytic-Synthetic and the Descriptive-Evaluative Distinctions," *JVI* vol. 3 (1969) 91.

90. KURTZ, P. "Has Ethical Naturalism Been Refuted?" *JVI* vol. 4 (1970), 161.

91. KURTZMAN, D. R. " 'Is', 'Ought', and the Autonomy of Ethics," *PR* vol. 79 (1970), 493.

92. LANGE, J. F. "R. M. Hare's Reformulation of the Open Question," *Mi* vol. 75 (1966), 244.

93. LEVI, A. W. "The Trouble with Ethics: Values, Method and the Search for Moral Norms," *Mi* vol. 70 (1961), 201.

94. LEWIS, D. "'Good' and Naturalistic Definitions," *An* vol. 24 (1963-4), 144.

95. McCLELLAN, J. E. and KOMISAR, B. P. "On Deriving 'Ought' from 'Is'," *An* vol. 25 (1964-5), 32. See (220).

96. McGUIRE, M. C. "Can I Do What I Think I Ought Not? Where Has Hare Gone Wrong?" *Mi* vol. 70 (1961), 400.

97. MACINTYRE, A. C. "Hume on 'Is' and 'Ought'," *PR* vol. 68 (1959), 451. See (220).

98. —— "Imperatives, Reasons for Actions and Morals," *JP* vol. 62 (1965), 513.

99. MACKENZIE, J. C. "Prescriptivism and Rational Behaviour," *PQ* vol. 18 (1968), 310.

100. MACKENZIE, P. T. "Fact and Value," *Mi* vol. 76 (1967), 228.

101. McNIVEN, C. D. "Analytic and Existential Ethics," *Dl* vol. 9 (1970), 1.

102. MADELL, G. "Hare's Prescriptivism," *An* vol. 26 (1965-6), 37.

103. MARGENAU, H. and OSCANYAN, F. "A Scientific Approach to the Theory of Values," *JVI* vol. 3 (1969), 162.

104. MARGOLIS, J. "The Analysis of 'Ought'," *AJP* vol. 48 (1970), 44.

105. —— "Classification and the Concept of Goodness," *AJP* vol. 41 (1963), 182.

106. —— "The Use and Syntax of Value Judgments," *JVI* vol. 2 (1968), 31.

107. MATTHEWS, G. "Weakness of Will," *Mi* vol. 75 (1966), 405.

108. MAVRODES, G. I. "'Is' and 'Ought'," *An* vol. 25 (1963-4), 42.

109. MISH'ALANI, J. K. " 'Duty', 'Obligation' and 'Ought'," *An* vol. 30 (1969), 33.

110. MITCHELL, D. "Must We Talk About 'Is' and 'Ought'?" *Mi* vol. 77 (1968), 543.

111. MITCHELL, D. "Some Comments on Ethical Distinctions," *PQ* vol. 13 (1963), 39.

112. MONRO, D. H. Critical notice of R. M. Hare's *Freedom and Reason, AJP* vol. 42 (1964) 119.

113. MONTAGUE, R. "'Is' to 'Ought'," *An* vol. 26 (1965–6), 104.

114. —— "The Literal Meaning of 'Good'," *An* vol. 24 (1963–4), 137.

115. —— "'Ought' from 'Is'," *AJP* vol. 43 (1965), 144.

116. —— "Universalizability," *An* vol. 25 (1964–5), 198.

117. MONTEFIORE, A. "The Meaning of 'Good' and the Act of Commendation," *PQ* vol. 17 (1967), 115.

118. MOORE, G. E. "A Reply to My Critics." See (241), (210).

119. MORRIS, W. E. "Professor Sen and Hare's Rule," *Ph* vol. 41 (1966), 357.

120. MURPHY, A. E. "John Dewey and American Liberalism," *JP* vol. 57 (1960), 420.

121. NAKHNIKIAN, G. "On the Naturalistic Fallacy." See (201).

122. NICHOLSON, P. P. "Mackenzie on Fact and Value," *Mi* vol. 79 (1970), 602.

123. NICKEL, J. W. "Hare's Arguments from Linguistic Change," *Eth* vol. 79 (1969), 298.

124. —— "Mr. Stearns on Naturalism," *JVI* vol. 3 (1969), 43.

125. NIELSEN, K. "Ethical Naturalism Once Again," *AJP* vol. 40 (1962), 312.

126. NOWELL-SMITH, P. H. and LEMMON, E. J. "Escapism: the Logical Basis of Ethics," *Mi* vol. 69 (1960), 289.

127. OLSCAMP, P. J. "Hare's Failure to Define Good Reasons," *Mi* vol. 79 (1970), 241.

128. —— "Infra- and Extra-Systematic Questions in Ethical Analysis," *PQ* vol. 5 (1965), 66.

129. OLSHEWSKY, T. M. "A Third Dogma of Empiricism," *Mo* vol. 49 (1965), 304.

130. PATTON, T. E. and ZIFF, P. "On Vendler's Grammar of 'Good'," *PR* vol. 73 (1964), 528.

131. PERRY, T. D. "Moral Autonomy and Reasonableness," *JP* vol. 65 (1968), 383.

132. PHILLIPS, D. Z. "Miss Anscombe's Grocer," *An* vol. 28 (1968), 177.

133. —— "The Limitations of Miss Anscombe's Grocer," *An* vol. 29 (1969), 97.

134. —— "The Possibilities of Moral Advice," *An* vol. 25 (1964–5), 37. See (220).

135. PHILLIPS, D. Z. and MOUNCE, H. O. "On Morality's Having a Point," *Ph* vol. 40 (1965). See (220).

136. PRIOR, A. N. "The Autonomy of Ethics," *AJP* vol. 38 (1960), 199.

137. —— "Escapism: The Logical Basis of Ethics." See (226).

138. RALLS, A. "The Game of Life," *PQ* vol. 16 (1966), 23.

139. REED, T. M. "The Implications of Prescriptivism," *PQ* vol. 19 (1969), 348.

140. ROBERTS, G. W. "Factual and Evaluative Statements," *JVI* vol. 1 (1967), 149.

141. —— "Hare on Ideals and Interests," *JVI* vol. 2 (1968), 201.

142. ROSEN, B. "Rules and Justified Moral Judgments," *PPR* vol. 30 (1970), 436.

143. RYAN, A. "Universalizability," *An* vol. 25 (1964–5), 44.

144. SCHRADER, G. "The Status of Value," *JVI* vol. 3 (1969), 196.

145. SCHWYZER, H. "Rules and Practices," *PR* vol. 78 (1969), 451.

146. SCOTT-TAGGART, M. J. "MacIntyre's Hume," *PR* vol. 70 (1961), 239.

147. SEARLE, J. R. "How to Derive 'Ought' from 'Is'," *PR* vol. 73 (1964), 43. See (220), (210).

148. —— "Meaning and Speech Acts." See (240).

149. SELLARS, R. W. "In What Sense Do Value Judgments and Moral Judgments Have Objective Import?" *PPR* vol. 28 (1967), 1.

150. SELLARS, W. "Imperatives, Intentions and the Logic of 'Ought'." See (201).

151. SEN, A. K. "Hume's Law and Hare's Rule," *Ph* vol. 41 (1966), 75.

152. —— "The Nature and Classes of Prescriptive Judgments," *PQ* vol. 17 (1967), 46.

153. SHAW, P. D. "Arguments from Fact to Value-Judgment," *PQ* vol. 18 (1968), 249.

154. —— "Ought and Can," *An* vol. 25 (1964–5), 196.

155. SLEEPER, R. W. "Dewey's Metaphysical Perspective: A Note on White, Geiger and the Problems of Obligation," *JP* vol. 57 (1960), 100.

156. SLOMAN, A. "How to Derive 'Better' from 'Is'," *APQ* vol. 6 (1969), 43.

157. —— "'Ought' and 'Better'," *Mi* vol. 79 (1970), 385.

158. —— "Transformations of Illocutionary Acts," *An* vol. 30 (1969), 56.

159. Entry omitted.

160. SLOTE, M. A. "Value Judgments and the Theory of Important Criteria," *JP* vol. 65 (1968), 94.

161. SMART, J. J. C. "Extreme and Restricted Utilitarianism," *PQ* vol. 6 (1956), 344. See (210), (249).

162. SNOOK, I. A. "Katz on 'Good'," *AJP* vol. 48 (1970), 120.

163. SOLOMON, R. C. "Normative and Meta-Ethics," *PPR* vol. 31 (1960), 97.

164. SPARSHOTT, F. E. Critical study of R. M. Hare's *Freedom and Reason*, *PQ* vol. 14 (1964), 358.

165. STACK, G. J. "Value and Fact," *JVI* vol. 3 (1969), 205.

166. STEARNS, J. B. "Evaluative and Supervenient Words: A Reply," *JVI* vol. 3 (1969), 46.

167. —— "A Refutation of Axiological Naturalism," *JVI* vol. 1 (1967), 117.

168. STEVENSON, C. L. "Moore's Arguments against Certain Forms of Naturalism." See (241), (210).

169. STIGEN, A. "Mrs. Foot on Moral Arguments," *Mi* vol. 69 (1960), 76.

170. STOJANOVIC, S. "Hare's Argument against Ethical Naturalism," *Mi* vol. 72 (1963), 264.

171. SUMNER, L. W. "Hare's Arguments Against Ethical Naturalism," *JP* vol. 64 (1967), 779.

172. —— "Value Judgments and Action," *Mi* vol. 77 (1968), 383.

173. TAYLOR, C. C. W. Critical Notice of R. M. Hare's *Freedom and Reason*, *Mi* vol. 74 (1965), 280.

174. TAYLOR, P. W. "Prescribing and Evaluating," *Mi* vol. 71 (1962), 212.

175. TEICHMANN, J. "Mrs. P. Foot on Morality and Virtue," *Mi* vol. 69 (1960), 244.

176. THOMAS, A. L. "Facts and Rudeness," *Mi* vol. 74 (1965), 399.

177. THOMSON, J. and THOMSON, J. J. "How Not to Derive 'Ought' from 'Is'," *PR* vol. 73 (1964), 512. See (220).

178. VEATCH, H. "Good Reasons and Prescriptivism in Ethics a Meta-ethical Impossibility?" *Eth* vol. 50 (1969–70), 102.

179. VENDLER, Z. "The Grammar of Goodness," *PR* vol. 72 (1963), 446.

180. WALLACE, J. D. "Anti-Naturalism," *Eth* vol. 78 (1967–8), 291.

181. WALTER, E. F. "Empiricism and Ethical Reasoning," *APQ* vol. 7 (1970), 364.

182. WELLMAN, C. "Emotivism and Ethical Objectivity," *APQ* vol. 5 (1968), 90.

183. WERNER, C. G. "Good and Obligation," *Eth* vol. 7 (1966–7), 135.

184. WHITE, H. J. "An Analysis of Hare's Application of the Thesis

of Universalizability in His Moral Arguments," *AJP* vol. 47 (1969), 174.

185. WILCOX, J. T. "Stevenson and the Referent of an Ethical Statement," *An* vol. 23 (1962–3), 58.

186. WILKINS, B. T. "The 'Is'—'Ought' Controversy," *Eth* vol. 80 (1969–70), 160.

187. WILLIAMSON, C. "The Grocers of Miss Anscombe and Mr. Phillips," *An* vol. 28 (1968), 179.

188. ZIMMERMAN, M. "The 'Is-Ought': an Unnecessary Dualism," *Mi* vol. 71 (1962), 54. See (220).

189. —— "A Note on the 'Is-Ought' Barrier," *Mi* vol. 76 (1967), 286. See (220).

B. BOOKS

190. ADAMS, E. M. *Ethical Naturalism and the Mordern World-View* (Chapel Hill, N. Carolina University Press, 1960).

191. AIKEN, H. D. *Reason and Conduct: New Bearings in Moral Philosophy* (New York, A. A. Knopf, 1962).

192. ANSCOMBE, G. E. M. *Intention* (Oxford, Blackwell, 1958).

193. AUSTIN, J. L. *How to Do Things with Words* (Oxford, Clarendon, 1962).

194. —— *Philosophical Papers* (Oxford, Clarendon, 1961).

195. AYER, A. J. *Language, Truth and Logic* (2nd edn) (London, Gollancz, 1956).

196. —— *Philosophical Essays* (London, Macmillan, 1963)

197. BAIER, K. *The Moral Point of View* (Ithaca, Cornell University Press, 1958).

198. BEARDSMORE, R. W. *Moral Reasoning* (London, Routledge & Kegan Paul, 1969).

199. BLANSHARD, B. *Reason and Goodness* (London, Allen & Unwin, 1961; New York, Macmillan, 1961).

200. BRANDT, R. *Ethical Theory* (Englewood Cliffs, Prentice-Hall, 1959).

201. CASTANEDA, H-N and NAKHNIKIAN, G. *Morality and the Language of Conduct* (Detroit, Wayne State University Press, 1965).

202. COHEN, M. R. *Reason and Nature* (Glencoe, Free Press, 1953).

203. DOWNIE, R. S. and TELFER, E. *Respect for Persons* (London, Allen & Unwin, 1969).

204. EDEL, A. *Ethical Judgment: The Use of Science in Ethics* (Glencoe, Free Press, 1955).

205. —— *Method in Ethical Theory* (London, Routledge & Kegan Paul, 1963).

206. —— *Science and the Structure of Ethics:* International Encyclopaedia of Unified Science, vol. II no. 3 (Chicago, Chicago University Press, 1961).

207. EDEL, M. and EDEL, A. *Anthropology and Ethics* (2nd edn) (Cleveland, Case Western Reserve University Press, 1968).

208. EDGLEY, R. *Reason in Theory and Practice* (London, Hutchinson, 1969).

209. EDWARDS, P. *The Logic of Moral Discourse* (Glencoe, Free Press, 1955).

210. FOOT, P. (ed.) *Theories of Ethics* (Oxford, Oxford University Press, 1967).

211. FRANKLIN, R. L. *Freewill and Determinism* (London, Routledge & Kegan Paul, 1968).

212. GAUTHIER, D. P. *Practical Reasoning* (Oxford, Clarendon, 1963).

213. GOTSHALK, D. W. *Patterns of Good and Evil: A Value Analysis* (Illinois, Illinois University Press, 1963).

214. HALL, E. W. *Our Knowledge of Fact and Value* (Chapel Hill, North Carolina University Press, 1961).

215. HAMPSHIRE, S. *Thought and Action* (London, Chatto & Windus, 1959).

216. HARE, R. M. *Freedom and Reason* (Oxford, Clarendon, 1963).

217. —— *The Language of Morals* (Oxford, Clarendon, 1952).

218. HARTLAND-SWAN, J. *An Analysis of Morals* (London, Allen & Unwin, 1960).

219. HARTMAN, R. S. *The Structure of Value: Foundations of Scientific Axiology* (Carbondale, Southern Illinois University Press, 1967).

220. HUDSON, W. D. (ed). *The Is/Ought Question* (London, Macmillan, 1969).

221. KATZ, J. J. *The Philosophy of Language* (New York, Harper & Row, 1966).

222. KERNER, G. C. *The Revolution in Ethical Theory* (Oxford, Clarendon, 1966).

223. KOVESI, J. *Moral Notions*, (London, Routledge & Kegan Paul, (1967).

224. LADD, J. *The Structure of a Moral Code* (Cambridge, Mass.; Harvard University Press, 1957).

225. MAYO, B. *Ethics and the Moral Life* (London, Macmillan, 1958).
226. MELDEN, A. I. (ed.) *Essays in Moral Philosophy* (Seattle, Washington University Press, 1958).
227. MONRO, D. H. *Empiricism and Ethics* (Cambridge, Cambridge University Press, 1967).
228. MOORE, G. E. *Principia Ethica* (Cambridge, Cambridge University Press, 1903).
229. NOWELL-SMITH, P. H. *Ethics* (London, Penguin, 1954).
230. PEPPER, S. C. *Ethics* (New York, Appleton-Century-Croft, 1960).
231. —— *The Sources of Value* (California University Press, 1950).
232. PERRY, R. B. *Realms of Value* (Cambridge, Mass.; Harvard University Press, 1954).
233. POLE, D. *Conditions of Rational Inquiry: A Study in the Philosophy of Value* (London, Athlone Press, 1961).
234. PRIOR, A. N. *Logic and the Basis of Ethics* (Oxford, Clarendon, 1949).
235. QUINE, W. V. *Word and Object* (Boston, M.I.T. Press, 1960).
236. RESCHER, N. *Introduction to Value Theory* (Englewood Cliffs, Prentice-Hall, 1969).
237. —— *The Logic of Commands* (London, Routledge & Kegan Paul, 1966).
238. RESCHER, N. (ed.) *Studies in Moral Philosophy* (*American Philosophical Quarterly* Monographs: Oxford, Blackwell, 1968).
239. RICE, P. B. *On the Knowledge of Good and Evil* (New York, Random House, 1955).
240. ROLLINS, C. D. (ed.) *Knowledge and Experience* (Pittsburgh University Press, 1962).
241. SCHILPP, P. A. (ed.) *The Philosophy of G. E. Moore* (Evanston, Northwestern University Press, 1942).
242. —— (ed.) *The Philosophy of Rudolf Carnap* (Illinois, Open Court, 1963).
243. SEARLE, J. R. *Speech Acts* (Cambridge, Cambridge University Press, 1970).
244. SINGER, M. G. *Generalisation in Ethics* (New York, A. Knopf, 1961).
245. SPARSHOTT, F. E. *An Enquiry into Goodness* (Toronto, Toronto University Press, 1958).
246. STEVENSON, C. L. *Ethics and Language* (New Haven, Yale University Press, 1944).
247. —— *Facts and Values* (New Haven, Yale University Press, 1963).

248. TAYLOR, P. W. *Normative Discourse* (Englewood Cliffs, Prentice-Hall, 1961).
249. THOMSON, J. J. and DWORKIN, G. (eds.) *Ethics* (New York, Harper & Row, 1968).
250. URMSON, J. O. *The Emotive Theory of Ethics* (London, Hutchinson, 1968).
251. VON WRIGHT, G. H. *The Varieties of Goodness* (London, Routledge & Kegan Paul, 1963).
252. WARNOCK, G. *Contemporary Moral Philosophy* (London, Macmillan; New York, St. Martin's Press, 1967).
253. WARNOCK, M. *Ethics since 1900* (Oxford, Oxford University Press, 1960).
254. WELLMAN, C. *The Language of Ethics* (Cambridge Mass.; Harvard University Press, 1961).
255. ZIFF, P. *Semantic Analysis* (Ithaca, Cornell University Press, 1960).

Cowardice and Courage

JAMES D. WALLACE

IT is difficult to do things which one believes to be dangerous, more difficult for some than for others. It sometimes happens, however, that the considerations in favor of a dangerous course of action make it seem worth the risks. People are sometimes able to act in the face of such dangers, but sometimes they are deterred. It might be that as the moment to act approaches, one's fear grows, and one becomes irresolute. Joseph Conrad, in Chapter I of *Lord Jim*, describes such a moment for a young man who dreamed of acts of unflinching heroism.

> He was jostled. "Man the cutter!" Boys rushed past him. A coaster running in for shelter had crashed through a schooner at anchor, and one of the ship's instructors had seen the accident. A mob of boys clambered on the rails, clustered round the davits. "Collision. Just ahead of us. Mr. Symons saw it." A push made him stagger against the mizzen-mast, and he caught hold of a rope. The old training-ship chained to her moorings quivered all over, bowing gently head to wind, and with her scanty rigging humming in a deep bass the breathless song of her youth at sea. "Lower away!" He saw the boat, manned, drop swiftly below the rail, and rushed after her. He heard a splash. "Let go; clear the falls!" He leaned over. The river alongside seethed in frothy streaks . . . Jim felt his shoulder gripped firmly. "Too late, youngster."

With cases of this sort in mind, we might construe courage as the ability to act upon one's beliefs about what it is best to do when fear inclines one not to act so. Courage, on this view, is a form of what Aquinas called "fortitude."

> . . . the passions withdraw us from following the dictate of reason, e.g., through fear of danger or toil, and then man needs to be strengthened for that which reason dictates, lest he turn back, and to this end there is *fortitude*. (*ST* I-II, Q61, art. 2)

On this view courage and cowardice have to do with the *conflict* of reason with the passion, fear. The conflict is envisaged as taking place within the breast of the agent.

On another possible view, however, courage is necessary in dangerous situations for proper practical reasoning; that is, where danger is involved, for properly grounded belief about what course of action is best, one needs courage. A coward, on the other hand, is someone

97

whose practical reasoning is defective in a certain way: In his deliberations, he gives too much weight to dangers to himself and as a result makes wrong decisions. One might say with Plato that a coward is ignorant of what is and what is not truly dangerous, and consequently he makes errors in weighing and measuring goods and evils in deliberations (*Protagoras*, 360 B-D).

On the first view of courage and cowardice, which I shall call the "Kantian" view (with apologies to Kant), a coward is prevented by fear from doing what he thinks best. Courage is the ability to do what one's reason dictates in the face of fear. According to the Platonic view of courage and cowardice, however, the coward gives too much weight to dangers in his calculations, and therefore he is deterred from a dangerous course of action when he should not be. Therefore, there is no opposition between what fear inclines him to do and the dictate of his reason. An adequate account of courage and cowardice must somehow combine elements of both of these views.

I

The relations between practical reason and fear are most easily seen in cowardly acts. It is instructive to take an ordinary uncomplicated act and consider what would have to be the case in order for the act to be cowardly. Suppose that a man named Smith stayed home today and his staying home was cowardly. It would have to be that his staying home today is incompatible with his doing something else which he has some reason to do. It would also have to be that he knows or imagines that there is danger involved in doing this other thing or at least that he is afraid to do it.

These two conditions are clearly not sufficient for the man's staying at home to be cowardly. Suppose he is a steeple jack staying home from work. Here, his staying at home is incompatible with his going to work, and he has some interest in going to work. His work is dangerous. Still, he might be staying home because he is sick or because he is lazy, and in such a case his staying home would not be cowardly. It would seem necessary to add that he is staying home rather than going to work because he is afraid to go to work.

Still, however, the description which has been given of Smith's staying home does not entail that his staying at home is cowardly. Suppose that his employer has altered working conditions so that Smith's work now involves a great deal of danger, and he is now staying at home because he is afraid to work under such conditions. Suppose that he is now expected to climb towers which are in danger of collapsing. It might be that he believes that working under such conditions is simply not worth the risk involved. Perhaps he does not need his present job enough to warrant taking such risks. If so, his staying home rather than going to work would not necessarily be cowardly.

From the foregoing, we might extract the following tentative list of necessary conditions for S's doing X to be cowardly:

There must be some action Y such that
(1) S is doing X rather than Y.
(2) S believes that he has some reason to do Y.
(3) S is doing X rather than Y because he is afraid to do Y.
(4) S does not *really* believe that his doing Y is not worth the risks it involves.

It is important to emphasize that in (4) we are concerned with what the agent *really believes*. In the grip of fear or agitation, one might sincerely avow things which one would reject in calm moments. Upon being shown instruments of torture by one's captors, it might seem to one that any betrayal is preferable to being tortured. If one believes this only because one is in the grip of fear, and if one would reject this in a calm moment, one does not *really* believe it. Also, S might pretend to himself that doing Y is not worth the risks it involves in order to avoid facing the fact that his act is cowardly. Someone really believes that p when he can sincerely avow that p in a calm moment without being guilty of self-deception.

That these four conditions are necessary conditions for a cowardly act is supported by the fact that if S does X rather than Y, and is accused of cowardice for this, S generally can turn aside the charge of cowardice if he can establish any one of the following.

(a) S saw no reason whatever to do Y.
(b) S's reason for doing X rather than Y was not that he was afraid to do Y; rather it was something else.
(c) S did X rather than Y because he was afraid to do Y, but S really believed that the risks involved in doing Y were not worth whatever good would be accomplished by doing Y.

Defense (a) entails the absence of necessary condition (2). Defense (b) entails the absence of (3). The latter is the sort of defense which a conscientious objector would be entitled to offer against the charge of cowardice. He might admit that he finds the prospect of fighting frightening, but that it is because of moral scruples about hurting people rather than fear of being hurt himself that he refused to fight.

There are often difficulties in actual cases in establishing that the facts which correspond to *a* and *b* actually obtain. Once established, however, those defenses effectively defeat the charge of cowardice.

Condition (4) and defense (c) which entails the falsity of (4) concern the relationship of practical reasoning and fear. If one takes the "Kantian" view that cowardice is a matter of fear overcoming an agent's practical reason, then one will expect that something like (4) is a necessary condition for a cowardly act. If from the start, both the agent's fear and his practical reasoning incline him in the same direction, there is no question of one overcoming the other. On the other hand, one might want to allow for the possibility that at least some cowardly acts result from an agent's giving danger to himself too much weight in his practical reasoning. If this is so, then (4) is not a necessary condition for a cowardly act, and there is at least some truth in the Platonic view.

Clearly, *some* cowardly acts are cases of fear leading someone to act contrary to what he thinks he should do, and in these cases, condition (4) is satisfied. In Conrad's *Lord Jim*, Jim's desertion from the Patna, a ship full of Moslem pilgrims for whose safety he was responsible, is one such case. The intensity of Jim's shame and remorse for his desertion shows that he believed that he should have stayed with the ship, yet he left because he was afraid for his life. This is one such case. Are there not cowardly acts where, although conditions (1)–(3) are fulfilled, the agent believes that doing *Y* is *not* worth the risk it involves? Jim was not the only officer of the Patna to desert the damaged ship and its passengers. The captain of the ship and some other members of the crew, whose duty lay with the ship as much as did Jim's, deserted also. Their crime, however, seems to have been something other than cowardice. In Chapter II, Conrad describes the passengers as they board the Patna at the start of the voyage.

> They came covered with dust, with sweat, with grime, with rags—the strong men at the head of family parties, the lean old men pressing for ward without hope of return; young boys with fearless eyes glancing curiously, shy little girls with tumbled long hair; the timid women muffled up and clasping to their breasts, wrapped in loose ends of soiled head-cloths, their sleeping babies, the unconscious pilgrims of an exacting belief.

The reaction of the captain of the Patna to this scene is, "Look at dese cattle." From this and other comments, it is clear that there is no doubt in the captain's mind that his passengers are not worth the risk of his own life. When he deserted the damaged ship in the face of a storm, he left because he feared for his life, but his desertion is due not to cowardice but to his callous indifference to his passengers and his indifference to the responsibilities of his position.

The case of the Patna's captain appears to support the view that (c) is a defense against cowardice and therefore the view that (4) is a necessary condition for a cowardly act. There are, however, two crucially different types of cases which fail to satisfy condition (4). One type of case, exemplified by the case of the Patna's captain, is not cowardly action. Another type, however, may be cowardly. Consider the case of Smythe who is terribly afraid of being hurt. He is convinced that it is worth suffering any frustration and humiliation in order to avoid the danger of pain and injury. He sometimes neglects his affairs, family, and friends, not because he is indifferent to these things. but because he is so afraid of being injured, that all other considerations pale beside the urgency of avoiding this sort of danger. Smythe's neglect of his affairs, etc., due to fear of injury might be cowardly, even though Smythe really believes that his affairs are not worth the risk of injury.

In the terms of condition 4, both the captain and Smythe have weighed the relative merits of doing Y against the risks. Both have decided that doing Y is not worth the risks. The difference between the two cases lies in the agents' attitudes towards the risks involved. The captain of the Patna has the usual fear of injury and death, but is relatively indifferent to the considerations which indicate his remaining with his ship. Smythe, on the other hand, has the usual concern for his affairs but seems *excessively* concerned about the possibility of being injured. He is excessively concerned because he is excessively afraid of being injured. It is because his weighing of the merits and risks is decisively influenced by his excessive fear that Smythe's staying at home is cowardly.

This raises the problem of explaining what it is to be *excessively* afraid. Following Aristotle, we might take as the norm the man who is good at deciding what to do—the man who is able consistently to make the right decision. *Excessive* fear would be that fear which led a person to give too much weight to danger in deciding what to do— more weight than a *phronimos* would give it. In the absence of an account of *phronesis*, however, this explanation is not very satisfying.

The norm relative to which excessive fears are excessive is to be found in our conception of normal human activity. Just as being injured and being ill are essentially certain sorts of incapacities for normal activity, so too is proneness to excessive fear. The capacities involved in being healthy (that is, being neither injured nor ill) are certain sorts of capacities for engaging in activities. These capacities involve having a body which will move in certain ways, a certain degree of strength and endurance, and the absence of pain which hampers activity. Certain states of the human body which appreciably diminish these capacities are illnesses and injuries. Being prone to excessive fear is like being ill or injured in that it incapacitates one, although the nature of the incapacity is different. For one thing, the incapacity due to excessive fear may be the result of one's giving too much weight to dangers in one's practical reasoning, whereas injuries and illnesses are not incapacitating because they distort one's calculations. The cause of the former incapacity is mental whereas the cause of the latter is physical. Being prone to excessive fear, however, is not necessarily a form of mental illness, although it may be if it becomes incapacitating enough. Just as too little strength and endurance may constitute a defect without being pronounced enough to constitute ill-health, so proneness to excessive fears may fall short of being illness.

The concept of *normal* human activity is extremely complex, and I mean only to refer to it, and not to explicate it. It is, however, a familiar concept; it is bound up in our understanding of health, illness, and injury, and, I am suggesting, our understanding of courage and cowardice.

The list of necessary conditions for S's doing X being cowardly, then, must be amended to allow for cowardly acts which do not spring from an opposition between an agent's reason and his fear. The first three conditions remain as before. That is:

(i) S is doing X rather than Y.
(ii) S knows or believes he has some reason to do Y.
(iii) S is doing X rather than Y because he is afraid to do Y.

The fourth condition, however, must allow for two different possible relations of S's fear and his practical reasoning. There are the cowardly acts in which the agent's fear opposes and leads him to act contrary to his practical reason. Such cases, exemplified by Conrad's Jim, support what I have called the "Kantian" account of cowardice. There appear to be cases, however, which do not fit this account; cases which seem to support the Platonic account. In these cases, the cowardly action issues from defective practical reasoning. Contrary to the account in the *Protagoras*, however, it is excessive fear, not ignorance, that leads the coward to give more weight to dangers than he should. The defect in his reasoning is not due to lack of information but to fear. Condition (4) for S's doing X being cowardly, then, might be reformulated as a disjunction.

(iv) EITHER *S* does not *really* believe that his doing *Y* is not worth the risks it involves, OR if *S* does believe this, he believes this because he is *excessively afraid* of the risks he sees in doing *Y*.

Conditions i–iv are intended to be necessary conditions for a cowardly act. Are they jointly sufficient? Since the first disjunct in (iv) simply states that the agent does not have a certain belief, it appears that all four conditions might be satisfied in a case in which S is undecided about whether the risk involved in doing *Y* is worth the benefits. It is doubtful that in *all* such cases *S*'s doing *Y* would be cowardly. People sometimes find themselves in complex and unusual situations where they must act quickly. In confusion and doubt, *S* might do *X* rather than *Y* because he fears the risks involved in doing *Y*, and he might have no idea whether his act is right or wrong. If *S*'s doubts and fears result from his being *excessively* afraid, that is, if but for his excessive fear, *S* would have seen that doing *Y* is worth the risks, then *S*'s doing *X* is cowardly. On the other hand, if *S* panics because of terrible danger, and his fear is not excessive, then his doing *X* because he is afraid to do *Y* may not be cowardly.

... there are things terrible even beyond human strength. These, then, are terrible to everyone—at least to every sensible man. . . . (NE 1115b 7–8)

It is possible to reformulate (iv) in such a way that cases in which *S* is prevented by a not-excessive fear from deciding whether doing *Y* is worth the risks can no longer satisfy this condition:

(iv′) EITHER *S* really believes that his doing *Y* would be worth the risks it involves, OR if *S* does not believe this, his not believing this is due to his being *excessively* afraid of the risks of doing *Y*.

Conditions i–iii and iv′ are necessary conditions for *S*'s doing *X* to be cowardly, but there are two sorts of circumstances in which all four conditions might be satisfied, yet *S*'s act not be cowardly. The first sort of circumstance is that described by Aristotle—the dangers in doing *Y* are "terrible beyond human strength," yet *S* believes that his doing *Y* would be worth the risks. The second sort of circumstance is that in which, although *S* thinks that doing *Y* is worth the risks it involves, really it would be foolish for *S* to do *Y* and face such risks. If *S* were to try to do *Y* but fail because he is afraid, it is not clear that his not doing *Y* is cowardly. Suppose, for example, that *S* wants to show off by playing a round of Russian roulette, but when he has pointed the gun at himself, he is too frightened to pull the trigger. It is not surprising that this sort of behavior is not regarded as cowardly, since here, rather than distorting his practical reasoning or preventing him from acting upon sound decisions, S's fear saves him from folly. Barring cases where the risks involved in doing Y are so terrible that no one could be expected to face them, and barring cases in which it would be foolhardy for S to do Y, if conditions (i–iii) and (iv') are satisfied, then S's doing X will be cowardly.

A coward, then, is someone whose excessive fears prevent him from acting upon his practical reasoning in situations where it would be neither foolhardy nor beyond human endurance to do so, or whose excessive fears lead him to give too much weight to dangers in his practical reasoning, thereby leading him to avoid actions which he would otherwise do. One's cowardice might be limited to certain sorts of dangers—one might, for example, be excessively afraid of physical injury, but not of censure, disapproval, or economic loss. A coward, however, is someone who is incapacitated.

II

The sort of courage which concerns us here is the courage which is the virtue corresponding to the vice, cowardice. It is the opposite of cowardice; the ability to weigh up correctly the pros and cons of various alternative courses of action when some courses involve danger and the ability to face dangers when this is indicated by practical reason. Courage and bravery are sometimes ascribed to individuals who bear up under grief and adversity, but we would not, I think, call someone a *coward* because he went to pieces in such circumstances. An exception to this is to be found in situations which confront a person with a fearful evil which he can in no way avoid. A person shows courage in facing his certain death with dignity and composure, whereas one who gibbers with fear might be thought to be cowardly. The kind of courage which is concerned with the facing of dangers where one has a choice in the matter generally involves the ability to master fear. This same fear-mastering ability is apt to be required to face certain death with composure, and one whose fear overcame him in the face of certain death might be presumed to lack the ability to face dangers where he might avoid the danger. The kind of courage which is most important and most useful, however, has to do with facing dangers where one has a choice in the matter. It is this which I will discuss.

Every courageous act must have some aim or end which the agent has reason to regard as important or worthwhile. Simply the fact that an act is a brave act, however, provides no clue as to what the aim of the act is or to what the agent's motive is. Some virtues are such that the acts answering to them must be done from a certain motive; for example, kindness and generosity. To be told that a certain act was generous is to be given some idea of the purpose or motive behind it, and sometimes no further explanation of the act is necessary. An example of this would be giving one's coat to a beggar on a generous impulse. People do not in the same way do things simply upon the prompting of courage. Courage, in this respect, is not motive. Courage is a virtue which is shown in acting for other ends and goals, but it is not itself a motive in the way that kindness or generosity is. One might do something in order to demonstrate one's bravery, but this does not make bravery a motive. Consider the fact that someone might do something to demonstate his generosity. It does not follow from this that his *motive* in doing this is generosity. In fact, it is hard to see how generosity could be his motive in such a case. Questions like "Why do that?", "What is the point of doing that?", and "What is his motive in doing that?" are not answered by pointing out that the act in question is brave.

Being kind, generous, or unselfish involves being likely to act from a certain sort of motive—wanting to help people and being willing to put oneself out to do this. Being brave, on the other hand, does not seem to involve acting from any particular sort of motives or for any particular ends, and consequently, one can act for motives that are morally reprehensible and still show courage. Protagoras, in Plato's dialogue by that name, may be right when he maintains that one could possess courage and none of the other virtues. Why could not a person be totally corrupt and insensitive, and at the same time be brave?

Courage is sometimes classified as a "self-regarding" virtue, as opposed to an "other-regarding" virtue, on the grounds that courage, like prudence, serves primarily the good of the courageous person himself. This is misleading, however. Kind and generous acts are necessarily intended to benefit another, and courageous acts are not *necessarily* so intended. On the occasions, however, when the good of others or the common good is or should be the decisive consideration in what one does, courage might very well serve the well-being of others. It is because a courageous person can be counted upon when the common good is threatened that courage is so prized. Prudence is essentially a virtue which concerns one's own crucial interests, and kindness is essentially concerned with others' well-being. Courage, like patience and industry, could serve the interests of the agent himself, but also the interests of others.

Since courage is the opposite of cowardice, there will be conditions

H

for courageous acts which are the counter-parts of the conditions for cowardly acts. Let us suppose that S does Y and the following conditions are satisfied.

(a) S believes that it is dangerous for him to do Y.

(b) S believes that his doing Y is worth the risks it involves.

(c) S believes that it is possible for him not to do Y.

Condition (a) is a necessary condition for S's doing Y being a courageous act. Someone who sees no peril in what he does is not acting courageously. The danger involved may be danger of injury or death for S or it may be danger of economic loss, loss of prestige, ostracism, or censure. Danger, here, is anything that threatens S's well being. If (a) is true, and S does Y, then S's action would be foolish or reckless if (b) were not true. Condition (c) requires that S think that he has some choice in the matter. When deep trenches are dug behind an army so that the army cannot retreat, then they are not being courageous when they stand their ground under attack.

Conditions (a), (b), and (c), however, are not jointly sufficient for S's doing Y to be courageous. Where the danger is slight and the reward substantial, doing Y will not necessarily be courageous. There is some danger involved in automobile travel, but people are not being courageous when they drive their cars. This suggests that the danger involved must be great enough so that it is difficult to do the act in question—not necessarily difficult for the agent, but at least difficult for most people. Aristotle says in the *Eudemian Ethics*:

> What, then, a coward as such fears is not formidable to any one or but slightly so; but what is formidable to the majority of men or to human nature, that we call absolutely formidable. But the brave man shows himself fearless towards these and endures such things, they being to him formidable in one sense but in another not—formidable to him *qua* man, but not formidable to him except slightly so, or not at all, *qua* brave. These things, however, are terrible, for they are so to the majority of men. (1228b 24–30)

This suggests still another necessary condition for a courageous act.

(d) The danger which S sees in doing Y must be sufficiently formidable that most people would find it difficult in the circumstances to do Y.

Some acts are more courageous than others. Just how courageous an act is depends upon how difficult it would be for us to face the danger it is supposed by the agent to involve.

Sometimes, however, when a person faces a danger of which he is terribly afraid, but which other people would not find formidable, we do see courage involved in his act even though condition (d) is not satisfied. He shows ability to master great fear, which is one of the capacities involved in courage, but his fear in the situation is excessive. The latter suggests that if the danger were increased a bit, then he would be too afraid to do Y, and his not doing Y would be likely to be cowardly. The two aspects of courage and cowardice—the "Kantian" or fear-mastering aspect, and the matter of feeling the appropriate degree of fear—conflict in such a case, and it is not surprising that we are pulled in two directions on the question of whether such acts are courageous. One might say in such a case that doing Y is brave *for the agent*, but it would not be correct to say unqualifiedly that his doing Y is courageous.

An agent, in performing a courageous act, need not feel any fear at all, nor need he find the act difficult. We admire the courage of someone who does something very dangerous so cooly that it appears to be easy for him. It is necessary, however, in order for an act to be courageous, that the agent be aware of the danger and that he recognize it as danger.

If conditions (a), (b), (c), and (d) are fulfilled, and the agent is *coerced* into doing Y, his doing Y may not be courageous. Aristotle remarks that soldiers who go into battle because they are threatened with terrible punishments if they refuse, show an inferior kind of courage. "One ought to be brave not under compulsion but because it is noble to do so" (*NE* 1116b, 2–3). These are cases in which a person faces danger because his only alternative is to face a different danger which he fears more. Now if a soldier's fear of fighting is excessive to begin with, so that he will not fight unless he is forced to do so, it is not surprising that his fighting under compulsion is not regarded as courageous. If one does Y because one is coerced by threats of terrible punishments if one does not do Y, then even though conditions (a)–(d) are satisfied, one's doing Y will not be courageous.

Apparently similar to the case of the soldier who fights because he fears punishment if he refuses is the following: A soldier fights because of his fear of being a coward, his fear of reproach both from others and from himself. Suppose that he would not fight but for his horror of being cowardly. It seems clear that his fighting may very well be brave. Why should fear of punishment disqualify an act from being brave, while fear of cowardice does not? There is this difference between the two cases: the second case, unlike the first, does not involve coercion. Why should this make any difference? A person who regards cowardly acts as shameful will thereby quite generally and systematically be strengthened for the dictates of reason in the face of danger. Someone might be brave without regarding cowardice as shameful, but the view that cowardice is shameful and the strong desire to avoid it clearly reinforces the effect of courage.

Another condition, then, for S's doing Y to be courageous rules out his being compelled by fear of punishment to do Y.

(e) S is not coerced into doing Y by threats of punishments which he fears more than he fears the dangers of doing Y.

There is at least one other condition which is necessary for an act's being courageous. We do not see courage exemplified in the actions of individuals who, because of frenzy, stupor, or intoxication, are not in control of themselves. Since courage is concerned with practical reasoning in the face of danger and acting upon the results of that reasoning, it is not surprising that we do not see courage in the behavior of someone whose powers of reasoning and apprehension are not functioning—someone who "does not know what he is doing" or who is not "in control" of himself.

III

The concepts of cowardice and courage, then, encapsulate the following suppositions. First, fear can prevent a person from doing what he thinks is best. Secondly, fear can lead a person to give too much weight to dangers in deciding what course of action is best. In this way, fear can disrupt one's practical reasoning, and it can prevent one from acting on the result of one's practical reasoning. When a person is such that in certain kinds of common situations, fear either distorts his practical reasoning so that he decides against dangerous courses of action which he would otherwise adopt, or fear prevents him from doing dangerous acts when he thinks this is best, then he suffers an incapacity. That is, there are things which people normally can do which such a person is barred from doing. In this respect, a coward is like a person who is injured or ill. Some people, on the other hand, have the ability to weigh courses of action involving danger without giving too much weight to the danger, and even to adopt courses of action involving danger in situations where the danger is so great that most people would have difficulty in managing their fear. Such people are courageous. The function of courage, then, is to preserve practical reasoning and enable it to issue in action in the face of danger.[1]

University of Illinois, Urbana-Champaign

[1] I wish to thank John Cooper and Louis Werner for helpful comments on earlier versions of this paper.

Injustice

A. D. WOOZLEY

ALTHOUGH philosophers and non-philosophers alike have written much about justice, they have not always observed the distinction between questions of analysis and questions of criteria, i.e., the distinction between what justice is and how to determine instances or non-instances of it. Thus, claims to characterize justice (a) in terms of fairness, and (b) in terms of equality are not merely different claims but claims of different kinds. That a given distribution is unequal among the recipients may be, and, depending on the context, is a good reason for saying that it is unfair, but it is not identical with its being unfair. We can ask whether a distribution is fair, and whether it is equal. But when we go on to ask why it is fair and why it is equal, we are asking questions that are very different from each other: in the first case we are seeking a justification of the claim that the distribution is fair; in the second case we are accepting that the distribution is equal, and seeking a justification of it being so. In short, even if it were true that the only way to treat men fairly is to treat them equally, treating them fairly, although it would consist in treating them equally, would not be conceptually identical with treating them equally. The core meaning of "fair" is a moral meaning, the core meaning of "equal" is not. "It is unfair to treat men unequally" is a significant assertion, and a moral assertion. "It is unequal to treat men unfairly" is not a moral assertion, and would need some torturing even to make into a significant assertion. And the proposition that all men are created equal is so conspicuously false if regarded as a factual proposition that it has to be interpreted as a moral proposition *about* equality if it is to have the ghost of a chance of being true, let alone be the self-evident truth that Thomas Jefferson proclaimed it to be.

Again philosophers have had comparatively little to say about injustice—which is surely the more interesting of the two. Here, perhaps, we have a case of what J. L. Austin used to call "trouser words," with "injustice" wearing the trousers. Justice is the least and the most anaemic of the virtues, about which it is difficult to get excited except where it is refused or threatened. We are liable to think of "unjust" as the contradictory of "just." Here we are wrong, for it is a contrary, but, as it is the only morally interesting contrary, the error is

109

understandable and has no serious consequences: it is not the absence of justice that we get excited about, but the absence of justice where it should be present. Failure to be just, not merely not being just, is what matters, and failure to be just is injustice.

We might start by saying that injustice is unfair discrimination between persons or classes of persons in the distribution of advantages or disadvantages, and that discrimination is unfair if and only if it is based on factors which are not relevant to the distribution. (This will soon need some qualifying.) The injustice of second-class citizenship consists in discriminating between whites and blacks, Aryans and Jews, in general A's and B's, where the dissimilarities between the A's and the B's, although they may be many, obvious, and considerable, are not relevant to the rights and capacities of citizenship; and it is not merely that there is nothing about white pigmentation or black pigmentation which is relevant, but that there is nothing about being a white or being a black which is relevant.

To justify something, such as a practice or an institution, is to show that it is right, or at least that it is reasonable to suppose it to be right; and one way of being right is to be just. But it is not the only way, for the just is a species of the right. It is further in my view possible (although many would dispute this) for a practice to be right, even although it is unjust. Treating people unjustly can sometimes be right and be shown to be right, to be justified in terms of social utility. Because "justify" has come to bear this wider meaning, of showing to be right (or, from another aspect, making right), we need another word with the more limited scope of showing to be just, or making just; perhaps "justicise" would do.

This first step of analyzing injustice as unfair discrimination, and unfair discrimination as discrimination based on factors not relevant to the distribution of the advantages or disadvantages involved, is only a first step.

Next, can we either list or give any general characterization of the factors which are relevant to questions of discrimination? Clearly they are factors about the patients in the case, those being treated unjustly, not factors about either the agents in the case or others who may be affected. If General Electric is treating its employees in Waynesboro, Virginia unjustly by paying them lower rates than it pays its employees in Schenectady, New York for doing exactly the same work, the injustice derives from facts about those employees, e.g., that neither the needs nor the merits of those in Virginia are different from those in New York; it does not derive at all from facts about the agent, e.g., that General Electric does not have to keep its wage rates

as low as job demand permits in order to stay competitive with rival
manufacturers; and it does not derive at all from facts about others
affected, such as the selling trade or the consumer. It may be unjust to
the latter that G. E. lower cost products from Virginia are sold at the
same price as the identical, but higher cost products from New York;
but, even if it is, then not reflecting lower costs of production in a
lower selling price is no part of the injustice to the employees at the
Waynesboro plant. This is the important distinction between "justify"
and "justice" coming in again. If G. E. can be charged with unjust
discrimination against its Waynesboro employees, it is not the beginning of a rebuttal for the company to say that it must keep wage rates
down to the lowest level that local conditions will permit—although
that might be the beginning of a rebuttal of the charge that is discrimination against Waynesboro employees is not justified. Again,
maintaining a uniform selling price to the trade may or may not result
in unjust treatment of the consumer, and it may or may not be justified.
But whether or not it is unjust to the consumer, and whether or not it
is justified, has nothing whatever to do with the question whether
paying a lower wage rate to employees in Virginia than to those in
New York is or is not unjust to the former.

As a beginning of a list of relevant factors, I have mentioned merits
and needs. I am sure they are both relevant, but I am not sure that
they are alike in the way that they are relevant. If a number of men
have equal needs, if you are in some way such as that of an employer
or a welfare agency responsible for meeting those needs, if you have
sufficient resources available to meet them, and if you then give some
men more than they need and (whether consequentially or not) others
less than they need, you are treating the latter unjustly. In that situation you have a double duty and they have a double right: you have
the duty to respond to their needs and the duty not to discriminate in
meeting their needs; and they have the two correlative rights. In the
case where you do not have the first duty you may still have the
second. Even if you do not have the duty to respond to their needs,
then, if you do respond to their equal needs but do not respond
equally, you are being unjust. Having a duty not to discriminate in
responding to equal needs does not imply having first a duty to
respond to the needs. A father does not have the duty to meet the
needs of his neighbor's children which he has to meet the needs of his
own; but if he does respond to the former, discrimination, if it leaves
the needs of some but not others inadequately met, is unjust. But the
principle of treating like cases alike, if it is not to be vacuous, needs
careful handling. If the needs of the recipients are equal, failure to

meet them equally is unjust. That is to say, a pattern of distribution which gave some more than they needed, but others less than they needed, would be unjust: the latter could justifiably complain that they had been treated unfairly. It is less obviously true that a pattern of distribution which gave some more than they needed, but none less than they needed, would be unjust. No doubt the latter would often protest that they had been treated unfairly, but it is not clear that they would be right; and, indeed, I do not think they would be. We thus have to distinguish between a weak version and a strong version of the principle of treating like cases alike.

Weak version. It is fair (not unfair) to treat like cases alike. This version does not entail that it is unfair to treat like cases unalike. Fairness permits the treating of like cases alike.

Strong version. It is fair (only fair) to treat like cases alike. This does entail that it is unfair to treat like cases unalike. Fairness demands the treating of like cases alike. The weak version clearly is true, i.e., it is never the case that it would be unfair to treat like cases alike. "Like" has to be understood as "relevantly alike": A's being like B in any old respect at all, regardless of the nature of the distribution, will not do. And equally clearly the weak version does not entail that it is unfair to treat like cases unalike. From the proposition that it is not unfair to treat like cases alike, nothing whatever follows about the unfairness (or fairness) of treating like cases unalike.

The strong version on the other hand, that it is only fair to treat like cases alike, clearly does have the entailment which the weak version does not: if it is only fair to treat like cases alike, then it is unfair not to, which is to say that it is unfair to treat like cases unalike. And it is the strong version of the "treat like cases alike" slogan which we are inclined to hold (of course it carries the weak version with it) and which we appeal to in what we think to be cases of injustice, viz., the injustice of treating like cases unalike. But, unless it is modified, the strong version is false: it is *not* always the case that it would be only fair to treat like cases alike—or that it would be unfair not to. If A's and B's needs are equal, then while it would be unfair totally to disregard that fact in making your distribution to them, it would not be unfair, having given equally to each what will satisfy his needs, then to give the whole of the surplus to A. B might protest that it was unfair that A got more than he himself did—many beneficiaries under a will have so protested—but he would be wrong, unless there was some further respect, other than need, in which B (possibly A also) had a claim on your distribution. If a father in the bequests which he makes to his two sons A and B has fairly met their needs, he does no injustice to *B* if he leaves the whole of the rest of the estate to *A*—unless there is some further respect, other than need, in which the distinction between like cases is unjust.

What this brings out is that the strong version is more complicated than the weak version. A modified strong version would be true, viz., that, if *A*'s and *B*'s needs are equal, it is only fair not to treat them as if they were unequal before reaching the point of meeting their needs. But the unmodified strong version summarized in the ambiguous slogan "treat like cases alike" is not true.

From Aristotle on it has seemed natural to think of injustice within the context of distribution of advantages or disadvantages (e.g., on the one hand emoluments, tax reliefs, exemptions; and on the other fines, taxes, military conscription), and of discrimination in the distribution which was not based solely on relevant factors about those who came out well or badly from the discrimination. This makes us think of injustice as something between the treatment of one individual and that of another, between the treatment of some individuals and that of others, between the treatment of one class and that of other classes, etc. The basic cry of injustice thus seems to be the child's "He has got more than I have" or "He has got one and I have not" or, on the other side of the account, "I was punished and he was not." It looks as if the only question we have is that of determining what are the justicising factors, of only one of which I have so far talked, viz., need. That is one question, but not, I think, the only one. There is also the question whether it is correct at all to define justice and injustice in terms of distribution and discrimination. I doubt whether it is; I do not doubt that the most conspicuous cases of injustice are those involving discrimination, but I am inclined to think that there is something more fundamental, that it is not so much the discrimination itself that is offensive as what is involved in the discrimination.

I find the second question more interesting than the first, the question of justicising factors, but I think the second can usefully be approached through the first. I am not going to attempt to make a complete list of justicising factors, but shall mention some that are commonly propounded and that have been held to be in one way or another relevant to the question whether discrimination is essential to injustice. The three sources that I have had primarily in mind are: Henry Sidgwick, *The Methods of Ethics* (6th Edition, 1901) Book III, Chapter V; A. M. Honoré, "Social Justice," *McGill Law Journal*, vol. 78 (1962) revised and reprinted in Robert S. Summers (ed.) *Essays in Legal Philosophy* (1968); and Nicholas Rescher, *Distributive Justice* (1966) Chapter 4. Not surprisingly, there is a high degree of agreement

I

between these sources (and others, too, which could be added) about the justicising factors. I give what is substantially, although not precisely, Honoré's list (not in his order):

1. Need
2. Desert—Achievement
3. Desert—Ability
4. Transaction
5. Special Relation
6. Conformity to Rule

In every case the person to be treated, justly or unjustly, has a claim on the agent, and the agent in not meeting the claim is guilty of injustice. This accords with the distinction made by Kant and again by Mill between justice and the rest of morals, the duties of justice being those which have correlative rights in the other party, other moral duties being those which do not: we have a duty to keep our bargains, e.g., contracts, wage agreements, conditions of service, etc. (= Honoré's *transactions*), and the other party has a right that we should; we may also have a duty of benevolence to others, but they have no right that we should be benevolent towards them. Failure in either would be moral failure, but only failure in the first would be injustice.

From the fact that we have a plurality of justicising factors it does not logically follow that there will be conflicts between them. It could be the case that they fell into an order which could be numbered from 1 to n, such that any factor outranked any other factor with a higher numeral; and I am not sure that Honoré, for example, does not believe that *need* outranks all the rest. But it seems to me clear that neither that particular claim, not the more general claim that some hierarchical ordering is possible, can in fact be sustained. And even under a single heading there can be conflicts, e.g., conflicting needs. Perhaps it is not necessary to stress that the issue is not always justice versus something else, say utility, but it seems at least worth pointing out, because in practical issues where questions of justice and injustice arise there is a human tendency to oversimplify. For example, in the school issue over busing children to achieve integration it is surely over-simple to suppose that justice points in one direction only. What follows in the remainder of this paper should be understood as being acknowledged to be subject to possible conflicts, not only between the different factors, but also under the heading of a single factor.

1. NEED

This is the factor which I have so far used in my examples, and I do not think more requires to be said about it now. If you have the duty of meeting needs, and you do not match distribution to needs, you are treating unjustly those to whom you give too little or nothing. We should distinguish between

(a) the criticism we might want to make of a society which, say, prefers to expend its wealth on missionary wars, or space spectaculars, or conspicuous consumption than on welfare and poverty programs,

and

(b) the criticism we might want to make of the inequitable legislation for, and operation of, welfare and poverty programs.

In (a) we are complaining about wrong priorities but not directly about injustice (although wrong priorities may breed injustice); in (b) we are complaining about injustice. Meeting the needs of some families, but failing to meet those of others, because they are hesitant to apply or ignorant how to, is clearly unjust. But even in this category of needs it should be noted that, although discrimination (whether intentional or negligent) nearly always is an element of the injustice, it does not have to be. The injustice of failing to pay a living wage is not conditional on discrimination, i.e., on paying some people better; it is possible to treat *everybody* unjustly by paying them less than they need. Fat cats among executives or stockholders are not necessary to the validity of a union's claim of injustice to the workers.

2. DESERT—ACHIEVEMENT

That a man has got less for what he did than he deserved, e.g., by way of payment or reward, or more than he deserved, e.g., by way of damages awarded against him or punishment, is perhaps the oldest cry of injustice. If not getting what you merited by your performance is not a paradigm case of injustice, what could be? Failure here is failure in Aristotle's distributive justice and the feeling for desert as a justicising factor is what lies at the root of objections to the views of penal and social reformers such as Barbara Wootton, who would have us in the area of crime give up thinking in terms of responsibility and punishment and think instead in terms of social utility. The objection to Barbara Wootton is less that for what he did the convicted man deserves to be punished than that he does *not* deserve to be submitted to therapy however securely beyond the stage of uncertain experiment the therapy may be.

Note that, as in the case of need, injustice in responding to the deserts of achievement does not require unjust discrimination, although very often that is the injustice that will be complained of. A man's getting less than he deserved for what he did is doubly unjust if somebody else got more than he, but it would still be unjust if nobody else got more, even if nobody else was involved at all.

3. DESERT—ABILITY

I have separated ability from achievement as a justicising factor (although neither Honoré nor Rescher does) because it seems to me far less clearly a justicising factor at all. They both find it unjust to a man to deny him what by ability he is qualified for; and so also does J. Feinberg in his "Justice and Personal Desert" (*Nomos*, vol. VI). Incidentally, being qualified must not be confused with being eligible. One can be well qualified, moderately well qualified, poorly qualified, etc.; and in considering rival candidates for an appointment, we *weigh* their qualifications. Eligibility, on the other hand, is an either/or, on/off business. I may be excellently qualified to be President of the USA, but I am not, and never can become, eligible; and of the millions of those who are eligible few are qualified. Again, the fact that I am qualified for a job is a good reason for appointing me (provided that, if there are eligibility conditions, I meet them); the fact that I am eligible for the job is, at most, a good reason for considering me. Nepotism in making appointments may be objectionable, but I doubt whether it is objectionable on the ground that it is unjust to the better qualified candidates for the job—unless other factors than simply ability are to be taken into account (as I think they normally are). If an employer in appointing a new secretary cares to disregard the excellent qualifications of Miss *A* in favor of the attractions of Miss *B* whose talents are strictly those of a businessman's playgirl, has he been unjust to Miss *A*? Not, I think, unless other factors are involved such as (1) a statement or an implied statement in the advertisement for the job that the candidate judged to be best qualified in secretarial skills would be appointed or (2) the existence of a convention or a rule that in competitive appointments the candidate judged to be best qualified is the one appointed. But then the injustice is, not failing to treat according to ability, but failing to act according to a specially or generally authorized expectation that you will treat according to ability. It can be imprudent not to appoint according to ability and it can be morally objectionable, but I doubt whether the moral objection can be that it is unjust *simpliciter* to disregard ability.

An objector might cite as counterexamples the injustice of denying civil rights to blacks or to women; that (to state the case at its mildest) plenty of blacks who have been prevented from registering as voters have been as well qualified to vote as plenty of whites who are registered; or that women have had it made difficult or even impossible for them to get into jobs and positions for which their ability is no less than that of male competitors. I do not deny the injustice of these examples, but I question whether they are always and clearly counterexamples. The fight for such rights has, on the whole, been the fight against discrimination, not the fight against nonrecognition of ability by itself. Nonrecognition of ability can be unjust, viz., where on the one hand the ability is claimed or is so conspicuous as to stand in no need of claiming and where on the other hand it is denied through hypocrisy or prejudice. What lies at the base of this is, I think, the injustice of affront or insult to which I shall be coming back shortly. The treatment of suppressed minorities (or majorities) whether they are blacks, women, Catholics in Northern Ireland, Jews in Russia, or whatever, is an affront in a way in which merely not to get a job because the boss has a weakness for dumb blondes is not.

I wonder whether the view that ability carries desert, which is a view that is widely held, with the consequences that it is unjust not to treat according to ability, does not perhaps rest on a confusion between ability and demonstration of ability. In many cases, where a choice has to be made between candidates, it is made on the basis of competition in a test or examination; and the choice is made on the performance or display of ability therein. If the man who has performed best does not get the job, he can protest at the injustice of it, because by his achievement, by his showing his superior ability, he deserved the job. There are, of course, possible complications to this: for example, it might be that, although A performed best, B showed more promise; in such a case it might be imprudent, or even wrong, not to appoint B; and, as showing promise is a way of showing ability, it might even be unjust to B not to appoint him. Again, B may have performed better than A over part of the examination, but not over the whole because he was taken ill during it, or from some other uncontrollable cause; in this case it might be unjust to B not to appoint him. And the method of selecting the performances that are to count as demonstrating ability may be open to criticism. This is especially liable to happen in situations where what matters is not just having an ability but also being on form or on a winning streak; for example, the method of selecting professional golfers either in this country or in Great Britain to play against each other in the Ryder Cup is frequently criticized on these grounds. But here it does seem to me more a matter of inefficiency or plain bad luck, rather than injustice. What is unjust is the denial of an asked-for opportunity to display an ability, if there is some evidence of its possession. So, it can be unjust to be refused an opportunity of displaying your ability, and it can be unjust not to be treated in accordance with your achievement in displaying it: but I am still unconvinced that it is unjust simply not to be treated in accordance with your known ability—unless, as I have hinted already, the failure to treat you so can reasonably be described in terms of affront.

4. TRANSACTIONS

The justice of transactions is approximately Aristotle's diorthotic justice: the justice of restoring the *status quo* exemplified by payment for services, compensation for harm done—and on the view generally taken by Anglo-American law that promises require consideration, the keeping of bargains and fulfillment of contracts. The injustice of transactions is simply the injustice of taking something for nothing, of getting something at somebody else's expense when he was not a willing party to your doing so. I have nothing more to say about it until I come back to asking whether there is any common thread running through the list of justicising factors.

5. SPECIAL RELATIONS

This is on Honoré's list but not on Rescher's. I am strongly disinclined to accept it. No doubt special relationships, contractual (e.g., husband-wife) familial (e.g., father-son), official (e.g., ruler, judge, policeman, etc., those over whom they have authority) and others produce special duties, but only where they also produce special rights do they make possible justice and injustice. A father who does not provide in his will for his son, where there is no special reason why he should not, may be open to moral criticism for not doing so, but unless the son has a claim under another heading such as need, or transaction, or rule, unfairness does not seem to enter into it. The special relations such as the contractual and the official that do make possible fair or unfair treatment clearly do fall under other headings, and I see no reason to retain this one. That the world would be a worse place if familial duties were not accepted and discharged is not identical with its being a more unjust place if they were not. Old people may be treated thoughtlessly, carelessly, heartlessly by their self-centred sons and daughters, but not in the absence of other factors unjustly.

6. CONFORMITY TO RULE

This either is itself or comprehends the most important factor of all. It is not merely that each of us has a claim that our society's rules should both be fair and be fairly operated, but also each of us has a claim that they should be observed. If the rule in question, whether being one of law, of positive morality, of custom, or of convention, serves a beneficial social purpose, it does so only provided that it is generally observed. For any individual to gain whatever advantages he does from breaking the rule or from treating himself as being exempt from it, it is in general necessary that others should not be breaking it: the situation has to be seen not just as the simple situation of A gaining an advantage by breaking a rule, but as the complex situation of A gaining an advantage by breaking a rule, which all (or most) others are keeping. Consequently the strongest argument against such a would-be rule breaker is neither that his conduct will, or is liable to, through its consequences undermine society (for in the case of most individuals its chances of doing so are negligible), nor that society would be undermined if everybody did the same (for it well might not), but simply the unfairness of his securing an advantage which depends on his breaking a rule in circumstances in which most others are keeping it. So the claim that we should conform to the rules does not depend on their being either legal or moral rules; it depends on those being the rules by which the game is being played. (It is not easy to be precise about what constitutes something being such a rule. But it can be as little as its being a matter of reasonable expectation, which is enough to create a rule, and to open the way for just and unjust treatment of others.)

What I want to suggest is that the notion (or notions) of reasonable expectations, or of the right to expect, is the basic notion of justice, and that injustice consists in treating people differently—more accurately, worse—than they have a right to expect. What treatment a man can reasonably expect, or has a right to expect, sometimes depends on the existence of rules, sometimes does not. We have thus two different types of case; we also have an ambiguity in "reasonable expectation" which we have to be careful about.

We can expect *that* people will in given circumstances behave in a certain way, and we can expect people in given circumstances *to* behave in a certain way; and expecting that they will . . . and expecting them to . . . are very different things.

(Certainly the range of use of each of these expressions does overlap the range of use of the other, so that within that overlap they are interchangeable; I am in this paper concerned with the non-overlapping portions of their respective ranges, e.g., the case where A can expect B to behave in a certain way at the same time as he cannot expect that he will.)

We can expect that people will behave in a certain way because there is a rule prescribing such behavior.

(a) At its weakest this is simply a regularity type expectation. We can and do expect that people will go on obeying this rule just because they always/usually have; or, as in the case of a new rule, we can expect that they will obey it because they always/usually have obeyed the rules. What makes this expectation reasonable or one which we have a right to or are entitled to hold is its inductive backing. (Note that "can" in "we can expect" does not mean "are able to" or even "are allowed to," but "are entitled to," "have a right to," "would be justified in," etc.) A simple illustration of the regularity type expectation (although not one depending on rules) would be that of Kant's neighbors setting their watches by his walking habits. These were so regular day after day that they could expect that they would continue, and they would be entitled to feel that something had gone wrong if he suddenly changed his walking schedule. They might feel, if they had really come to rely on his walking habits to determine the accuracy of their watches, that he had let them down if he suddenly changed, although they would not be *entitled* to feel so if there was nothing more to their relationship with Kant than I have supposed. They would be in the same position as the son who received far less under his father's will than he had counted on getting (provided, that is, that his counting on getting much more had been based just on evidence and not at all on promises or even strong hints by the father).

(b) Then we can introduce the notions of people accepting a rule, of feeling committed to it, or feeling bound by it. These are notions which are perhaps different from, although related to, each other. The differences do not matter to the present topic so I will use "feeling bound by" to stand for them all. We can expect that people will behave in a certain way as prescribed by a rule, not just because they always/ usually have, but because we can expect them to feel bound by it, and consequently because we can expect them to behave as prescribed. We are entitled to expect them to behave that way, or to demand that they should, for various possible reasons such as undertakings given, explicitly or implicitly, or society's dependence on reciprocity of sacrifice. Expectation that they will behave in the prescribed way is vulnerable to counterevidence, but expectation-to is not, or not directly, since it can be vulnerable to counterevidence showing *incapacity* to behave that way. We can have evidence about their past conduct or about their present plans and intentions such that we cannot expect that they will keep to the rule; but consistently and simultaneously with that we can expect them to keep to the rule. And in the absence of such counterevidence we can expect that . . . because we can expect them to. . . .

(c) Thus we can expect a man to behave in a certain way even though we cannot expect that he will because we know too much about him for such an expectation to be reasonable. A demand on a person does not fail to be reasonable just because the expectation that he will meet it fails to be reasonable. Because what we can expect a man to do is what we can rightfully demand of him, not only are there situations in which we can expect him to do what we cannot expect that he will do, but also there are situations in which we can expect that he will do what we cannot expect him to do. Kant's neighbors again illustrate the latter: they could expect that Kant would stick to his walking habits but they could not expect him to stick to them. They would not be entitled to complain of his letting them down if he suddenly changed his schedule; for them to be entitled to complain, not only would Kant have to know that they were relying on him as their watch-regulator, but they would have to know that he knew, and he would have to know that they knew that he knew.

The claim of justice within the context of rules is the claim that reasonable expectations of conformity to rule should not be disappointed. And the basic claim is that of expectation to, which may range up from expecting a man, or an official, or a government, etc., not to depart from the regularities and customs upon which we are known to be depending, to expecting him or them to behave in the way prescribed by the rule because he or they can be expected to feel bound by it. Injustice consists in failing to treat the victims of it in the way in which they can expect to be treated, at the same time, perhaps, as treating them in exactly the way in which they can expect that they will be treated.

This can be generalized to any case where one can expect to . . . including, that is, cases where even in the absence of rules one can expect to. . . . And there certainly are such cases. I can expect A to keep his promise to do x because he authorized me to expect that he would. The fact that by promising he authorized an expectation is the reason why he has the obligation to do what he promised to do. His obligation is not logically dependent on promises being a practice (in J. Rawls's sense), although the fact that they are such a practice may reinforce the obligation. Breaking a promise is unjust because it is somehow an affront or an insult to the promisee as a human being, in this case the insult of first conferring a right on him and then behaving as if you had not, and that I suggest is what injustice fundamentally is—the affront done to a man as a human being by not treating him in the way that he can expect to be treated. It is, I suspect, no accident that it is indignation rather than merely anger that we feel at injustice, whether we or others are its victims, and that indignation is still true enough to the etymology of the word to be dependent on viewing the treatment that arouses our indignation as somehow belittling or affronting the worth of the victim. Even where we are justified in treating people unjustly (and unhappily we sometimes may be) we are not to be admired for growing the calluses which make us insensitive to the affront we are doing them. The injustice which is done by discrimination when it is unjust (and not all discrimination is unjust) is the insult given to those discriminated against, the insult being rubbed in by letting them see others not relevantly different being better treated. The injustice done to women or to blacks does not absolutely consist in, although it is compounded by, their being discriminated against; the injustice is the insult of being held to lack the capacity or the qualifications which they clearly do not lack.

It is an affront to have a crying need denied or ignored, to have shown your worth by achievement and to have it belittled. It is inefficient, and socially wasteful, not to treat people according to their abilities, but it is not obviously unjust, unless on other grounds they could expect to be so treated. What is insulting about discrimination against, for example, women or blacks is not so much the failure to allow them to develop and exercise their abilities as the implied denial that they possess them. The boss who employs dolly girls rather than competent stenographers simply because he finds the former easier to look at is not being unjust to the latter; he would be, if he pretended that they were not as good stenographers as the dollies, and gave that as his reason for not employing them.

In this paper I have said nothing about canons or maxims of justice and injustice. I have been concerned solely with making some suggestions about the notion of justice, or rather the notion of injustice, itself. It seems advisable to be clear about that before going on to discuss the practically more demanding and emotionally more charged questions about canons. It may, for instance, be true that justice demands equality; but that truth, if it is one, should not be confused with the falsehood that justice *is* equality.

University of Virginia

INDEX OF NAMES